Reconnect to God with Ho'oponopono

Jimmy Scott

Kingdom Publishers

Copyright© Jimmy Scott 2024

All rights reserved. No part of this book may be reproduced in any form by photocopying or any electronic or mechanical means, including information storage or retrieval systems, without permission in writing from both the copyright owner and the publisher of the book. The right of Jimmy Scott to be identified as the author of this work has been asserted by him in accordance with the Copyright, Designs and Patents Act 1988 and any subsequent amendments thereto.

A catalogue record for this book is available from the British Library.

All scripture quotations have been taken from the *New International, New Living Translation, English Standard, New American Standard, and the Holman Christian Standard* Versions of the Bible

ISBN: 978-1-916801-02-8

1st Edition 2024 by Kingdom Publishers, London, UK.

You can purchase copies of this book from any leading bookstore or email **contact@kingdompublishers.co.uk**

"I am what I am by the grace of God, and by that alone"

(Augustus Toplady)

Dedications

My sincere thanks and appreciation to my family who provide the love and support to grow in life.

Specifically my loving wife Anne-Marie, you are my rock, I am so fortunate we share our devoted values !

Contents

Foreword	10
We continue...	16
Introduction	23
Why we should *want* to connect to God	26
▪ Practical and Cognitive reasons	28
• God is our Foundation	28
• God keeps us grounded	28
▪ Sense of purpose	29
• Spiritual growth	30
• Moral guidance	30
• Provision and protection	31
• We *need* spiritual contentment	32
• Knowing God builds courage, faith and strength	33
• Only by knowing God, can we know how to live	33
▪ A personal intimate relationship with the living God	34
• We *need* Salvation	35
• We should know Him	37
▪ Our connection with God is what makes us Christian	38
What the Bible says about connecting to God	39
The importance of sustaining a connection with our God	48
▪ Connecting with God provides guidance and direction	48
▪ Connecting with God purifies the Soul	49
▪ Our connection to God leads to *more* in life.	50

- Reconnecting strengthens our Faith — 51
- Eternal life is only possible through a connection with God — 52
- Connecting with God focuses our mind and thoughts — 52

What is Ho'oponopono ? — 54

Reconnect to God with Ho'oponopono — 63

- Statement 1: "I love you" (Adoration/Reverence) — 65
- Statement 3: "I am sorry" (Repentance/Atonement) — 79
  - Take Ownership — 81
  - Repent 88 — 82
  - Commit to Change — 83
  - Follow through — 85
- Statement 4: "Thank you" (Thanksgiving/Gratitude) — 89
- Statement 5: "Clean, clean, clean" (Wash away, cut the cord) — 94

How and when to use the Ho'oponopono statements/prayer practically? — 98

What to expect when Re-Connecting to God — 102

- A constant awareness of God's presence, with a deep sense of intimacy — 102
- Inner peace and harmony — 103
- Improved relationships — 104
- Physical and emotional healing — 105
- Increased spiritual connection — 106
- Greater clarity and purpose — 106
- Increased inner peace and happiness — 106
- Spiritual growth and transformation — 107
- Experiencing Gods love — 107
- Clarity of mind — 107

Security and contentment	108
Remaining re-connected to God	109
▪ Practice regularly	109
▪ Create an Atmosphere to Hear from God	110
▪ Cultivate positive thoughts and emotions	112
▪ Practice forgiveness	112
▪ Engage other forms of connection	114
▪ Take in the sights, sounds and smells of our surroundings	116
▪ Practice gratitude	117
Going Forward	119
▪ Take responsibility	119
▪ Be open to the guidance, wisdom and messages that God communicates to us	120
▪ Have passion in our endeavour	121
▪ Have Faith	123
To finish off…	126
References	133

Foreword

A few years ago, a group of colleagues and I engaged in discussions about the abundance of spiritual and self-help books flooding the market at the time. Despite most of us identifying as fringe Christians since our teenage years, we found ourselves readily drawn to the *new age* mind-set, at the time exploding onto the market with The Secret by Rhonda Byrne. The book (and movie) ostensibly based on views originally popularised by positive psychology writers such as Mihaly Csikszentmihalyi, Norman Peale and Ed Diener, literally took the world by storm with its new approach to achievement. The Secret ostensibly explains how the law of attraction, which states that positive energy attracts positive things into your life, governs our thinking and actions, and how we can "...use the power of positive thinking to achieve anything you can imagine" (Niklas Goeke, 2008; the Secret book and film have grossed over $300 million).

Despite being spurred on by fellow self-help writers such as Napoleon Hill, Tony Robbins, Deepak Chopra, Eckhart Tolle, Stephen Covey, Neville Goddard, M. Scott Peck, Esther and Jerry Hicks, Wayne Dyer, Neale Donald Walsch, Louise Hay, Sam Harris, Joe Vitale, and Gary Zukav, I gradually began to feel disconcerted and started questioning the true meaning of life. Although the new age philosophy was intriguing and illuminating, I sensed that there was still something lacking.

Having devoured countless books on spirituality and self-help, and spending a considerable amount of money in the process, I eventually returned to what I considered to be the fundamental approach of understanding life on Earth: through scientific, philosophical, religious, or individual beliefs. However, even after delving into philosophical and science works, I realised that although they provided explanations for many things and was advancing rapidly, they did not offer all the answers to my questions. Approaching life from a more personal perspective, I explored psychological, astronomical, and botanical viewpoints, which helped me manage some parts of life a little better, but still left me feeling unfulfilled.

Despite this, I persisted in my search and eventually turned to religion, delving into critical summaries of sacred texts such as the Tipitaka, Sutras, Vedas, Kojiki, Quran, Torah, and the Bible. It was during this process that something miraculous happened - while reading the first chapter of the Bible, the Holy Spirit told me unequivocally: *Welcome back, I want you to write; to spread the word*... even though I had never written anything of significance before.

After much reflection, I came to the realisation that it was important to raise awareness about the potential dangers of relying on self-help methods and to reintroduce the importance of living a life guided by God's teachings. Self-help is a process of improving oneself or overcoming one's problems without external assistance:

> "*A focus on self-guided, in contrast to professionally guided, efforts to cope with life problems, emphasising self-reliance, in which one addresses such problems on one's own e.g. by reading self-help books*" (APA, n.d.)

The self-help industry has become a lucrative business, in 2019 being valued at $10 billion in the US alone (Gitnux, 2023), and is growing rapidly – despite the industry being largely unregulated, filled with outmoded advice, and usually not scientifically validated.

The major issue with the self-help industry is that it can lead people away from the truth and create unrealistic expectations, which can result in a sense of false hope and achievement. As example, research has shown that those who prioritise extrinsic goals such as wealth may be at a higher risk of anxiety and depression (for more on this see Ettman, Cohen & Galea, 2020; & Ryu & Fan, 2023).

The self-help industry makes use of affirmations that promote positive thinking, abundance and confidence.

Here are some examples of such affirmations, please note the emphasis on the 'self':

- I have faith that the world will help me live my best life.
- I am strong and resilient, and I can overcome any obstacle.
- I am valuable and worthy, simply because I exist.
- I am proud of myself for all that I have accomplished.
- I am deserving of respect and kindness from others and myself.
- I am deserving of success and abundance in all areas of my life.
- I believe in myself and in my abilities.
- I am constantly attracting positivity and abundance into my life.
- I am capable of creating a life that brings me joy and fulfilment.
- I am committed to being at peace within myself and with everyone around me.

- I am my biggest supporter.
- I treat others and myself with kindness.
- I possess the power to manifest the life of my dreams.
- I am capable of making it all happen.

As seen from the above list, the common theme in self-help literature is that our thoughts and beliefs shape our experiences and realities. This concept is often referred to as the *law of attraction* or the *power of positive thinking* and the philosophy is that if we focus our thoughts and emotions on positive outcomes, we can manifest those outcomes in our lives. In other words, by shifting our mind-set and beliefs, we can create a more positive and fulfilling life for ourselves.

However, when we attempt to replace ourselves with something else, we are unlikely to succeed and may become susceptible to this pseudoscience and false claims that allow us to avoid dealing with our feelings of inadequacy.

As psychology researcher William Tov (2018) explained:

> *"The complexity of scientific research gets minimised in self-help books as people are not trained to interpret statistics and empirical research. People think they are getting really good advice from research, but not everything works for the same person. Change will take time and work but people are often seeking for a clear and easy solution through self-help books. So be aware of your biases like the confirmation bias. We tend to believe in any claims that are consistent with our general beliefs and, the trick is, we usually do not question that. We do not ask for further evidence. So, when authors make a strong*

recommendation or definite advice, critical thinking will help fight these kinds of biases. Ask yourself, 'How does this person know?' and fact-check with scientific sources wherever possible."

This does not mean self-help books and media are all bad. Some offer helpful insights on how to relate to others and set healthy boundaries on our time and with our money. However, if our first instinct is to turn to self-help rather than seeking guidance from Jesus, we are missing out on the ultimate source of help. Depending solely on our own abilities and relying on self-reliance is not the answer. Rather, we should turn to God for help whenever we need it, trusting in His power and guidance to provide what we truly need. Rather than seeking quick fixes and temporary solutions, turning to God allows us to find true and lasting peace and fulfilment.

Why not, we have the best book on the market, one that has sold more copies than any self-help book ever has. The Bible offers us guidance, wisdom, and truth that can provide us with the ultimate help we need. It is important to note that the Bible is not just a collection of self-help advice or a manual on how to live a good life. Instead, it is a collection of God's words to humanity, providing us with the key to unlocking our true potential as individuals created in God's image.

The Bible provides us with the answers to life's biggest questions and can guide us in our daily lives, giving us hope, strength, and purpose. By turning to the Bible, we can find the true source of help and the guidance we need to live a fulfilling life.

> *All Scripture is inspired by God and is useful to teach us what is true and to make us realise what is wrong in our lives. It corrects us when we are wrong and teaches us to do what is right* (2 Timothy 3:16 NLT)

Each and every word of the Bible is an extension of God's will, formed out of His spirit, in written form. Scripture is beneficial for teaching; good for exposing or pointing out sin; useful for correction; and guidance for training in righteousness. Though Scripture we learn what is true, what is wrong, how to correct wrong, and how to apply truth.

It's important to remember that our journey with Christ is just that – a lifelong process of growth and transformation resulting in a deepening relationship with God, a continual surrender of our will to His, and a willingness to follow His guidance even when it is difficult or uncomfortable. We will experience ups and downs, successes and failures, but through it all, God is faithful and will continue to work in us to make us more like His Son, Jesus Christ. So, turning to Christ offers something far greater than self-help books - a path towards true healing, wholeness and love.

We can and should rely on God, not on ourselves, to give us the help we need:

> *"Self-righteous striving is more hopeless than you want to believe, but grace is more life-transforming than you realise."* (Ruth Chou Simons, 2021:4)

Over the next few pages, we will venture into the world of Ho'oponopono and get into the why and how I have written this book.

We continue...

During my research in seeking answers to life, I quickly came to realise that philosophies of life are often strikingly similar in nature, regardless of where they originated around the globe. An example is an ancient traditional Hawaiian practice of conflict resolution and forgiveness that comprises bringing together individuals or groups to address and resolve disagreements or issues. Known as *Ho'oponopono,* it roughly translates as: to *make right or to correct* in Hawaiian. *The practice* involves a process of open communication and discussion, with the goal of reaching a resolution that is satisfactory to all parties involved.

Ho'oponopono involves a series of steps, such as expressing remorse, making amends, and seeking forgiveness, which are designed to restore balance and harmony to relationships. The traditional practice of Ho'oponopono is typically conducted by a trained elder or spiritual leader who leads a group of family or community members through a process of open communication and discussion in an attempt to address and resolve disagreements. The specific process typically involves each participant taking turns to share their thoughts and feelings, with the intention of fostering understanding, empathy, and forgiveness.

The ultimate goal of Ho'oponopono is to restore balance and harmony within the group or community by resolving conflicts and healing emotional wounds and with their relationship with God. (More about Ho'oponopono to follow)

Dr. Ihaleakala Hew Len, a clinical psychologist, reportedly employed an abbreviated form of Ho'oponopono while working in a state mental health clinic in Hawaii. He is said to have successfully worked with mentally ill patients who were beyond help from other clinicians, by focusing on his own thoughts and emotions and using the principles of Ho'oponopono to heal himself and his perceptions of the patients. Dr. Len's approach, which he called *Self-I-Dentity through Ho'oponopono,* was based on the idea that all problems arise from the memories and programs in our subconscious mind, and that by taking responsibility for those memories and programs and working to release them, we can experience greater peace and harmony in our lives.

In his work at the hospital, Dr. Len purportedly reviewed the medical charts of his patients and used Ho'oponopono to clear his own negative thoughts and emotions related to the patients and their conditions, with the intention of contributing to their healing. It is reported that during Dr. Len's residency at the hospital, the ward where he worked saw a significant improvement in the mental health of the patients. Some patients were even released from the hospital after being considered *cured*, while others showed notable improvement in their behaviour and demeanour. While his methods are not universally accepted in the field of psychology, his work has been influential in spreading awareness of Ho'oponopono and its potential applications in modern life.

Joe Vitale, a modern-day self-help author and speaker, further popularised the use of Ho'oponopono as a tool for attracting abundance and prosperity. In his book *Zero Limits*, Vitale's version of Ho'oponopono emphasises the cleaning of the subconscious mind of negative thoughts and beliefs. His approach is to take responsibility for one's own thoughts and actions, and to ask the self for forgiveness for any negative thoughts or emotions that may be contributing to feelings of stress, anxiety, or unhappiness. By taking responsibility for our own negative thoughts and emotions, we can clear them from our subconscious mind and transmute them into positive energies.

The process involves recognising that our negative thoughts and emotions are rooted in the past, and that by acknowledging and releasing these toxic memories, we can shift our energy towards a more positive and abundant state. Vitale's interpretation of Ho'oponopono has been exceptionally influential in the self-help and personal growth communities, and has been the subject of much discussion and debate among practitioners. Other authors that explore similar approaches include *Ho'oponopono Secrets* by Paul Jackson; *The Easiest Way* by Mabel Katz; *Ho'oponopono* by Ulrich E. Dupree; and *The Book of Ho'oponopono: The Hawaiian Practice of Forgiveness and Healing* by Luc Bodin & friends.

This book that you are reading, builds on the ancient concept of Ho'oponopono and its original aim: to re-connect with God. According to traditional Hawaiian spirituality specialists, Ho'oponopono is a practical and effective way to re-connect with God, bringing balance and harmony to life. The practice is based on the belief that everything in nature is interconnected, and that resolving conflicts and promoting forgiveness within oneself and with others is necessary for achieving peace and well-being with God. Therefore, the goal of Ho'oponopono is to restore our balance and harmony with God and to promote inner peace and well-being.

By employing the Ho'oponopono process, individuals can work to resolve conflicts and repair relationships, both with others and within themselves, and with their Creator. Hence, Ho'oponopono leads us to spiritual practices that help us to deepen our connection with God and to live in greater harmony with God's will.

The reason for writing this book is that it provides a practical and effective way to regain our connection with our Creator and achieve greater meaningfulness in our lives. The idea is for us to become fully centred and awakened in a state of balance and harmony, both within ourselves and with the world around us, with the joy and comfort we experience with the deep sense of connection with God. By doing so, we can find a sense of purpose and direction in our lives that transcends the mundane and allows us to live with greater meaning and fulfilment.

The original Hawaiian Ho'oponopono philosophy states that:

- God is our redeemer
- Everything and everyone is connected
- We are responsible for our actions
- We need to own up to our transgressions
- Forgiveness is critical for life to go on
- Open, honest communication is paramount

This philosophy, along with Dr Len's *Self-I-Dentity* approach of self-responsibility determining outcomes is melted together with Joe Vitale's, *Zero Limit*, four phrases of *I am sorry, Please forgive me, Thank you* and *I love you*, to form a mantra and rationale for us to employ in a cognitive and Godly manner. The result is a sure-fire cognitive means for us to re-connect to our Lord Jesus Christ.

In this book, I try keep the nomenclature equal between the Trinity of God the Father, God the Son (Jesus) and God the Holy Spirit (and sometimes the Divine, His, Him). God is the ultimate Supreme Being who is Omnipotent (God has the power to do anything); Omniscient (Jesus is all knowing, nothing is hidden or beyond comprehension); Omnipresent (The Holy Spirit is present everywhere, always); and Eternal (God is without beginning, or end).

God is the Creator of the universe, the source of all life and provides for us. Jesus Christ is the Son of God who was sent to earth to save humanity from sin through his teachings, crucifixion and resurrection. Jesus is the only way to salvation, and by believing in him and following his teachings, we are saved to enjoy eternal life with God. Jesus now lives at the right-hand side of God in Heaven.

> ***I am the way, the truth and the life. No one comes to the Father except through me.*** *(John 14:6)*

Jesus shed His own innocent blood as full and final payment for all the sins of the world, offering us eternal life - without the shedding of blood there simply is NO redemption!

The Holy Spirit is the active presence of Jesus Chris in the world, guiding and empowering believers to do His work. This is further depicted in the figure below, which displays the interaction of God the Father, God the Son and God the Holy Spirit in Holy Trinity.

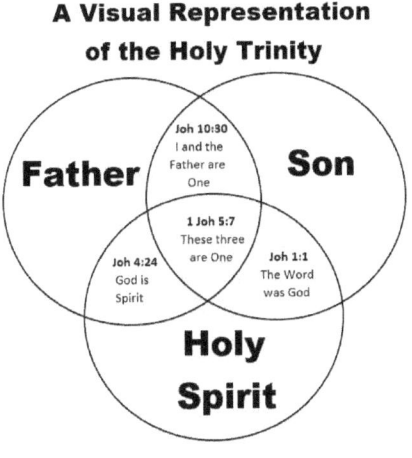

(by Ken Everett, 2020)

The Holy Bible depicts all three entities of the Trinity as: each is separate and distinct; each is equal to one another; and yet all work together and are fused as one (1x1x1x = 1). David Pawson describes this as *Triunetheism* where God is three in one, creator and controller of the universe. Billy Graham adds to this and states: "God the Father is fully God; God the Son is fully God; and God the Holy Spirit is fully God" (Graham, 1978:16). Thus, we say that we pray to the Father through the Son and in the power of the Holy Spirit.

> *The grace of the Lord Jesus Christ, and the love of God, and the fellowship of the Holy Spirit, be with you all.*
> (2 Cor. 13:14)

Paul's benedictions specifically reference all three members of the Trinity. These are the Lord Jesus Christ who died for our sins on the cross; Father God who sent his son Jesus Christ to earth to ensure the forgiveness of sin is possible; and God's Holy Spirit who makes it possible for us to communicate with the Father while we await the Second Coming.

This book is written for Christians, but can as easily be understood and followed by worshippers of any other spiritual entity. The important message is that the Ho'oponopono mantra is an effective method to re-connect with God. The mantra involves the critical parts of any reconnection and reconciliation message, namely: Adoration/Reverence, Supplication/Petition, Repentance/Atonement and Thanksgiving/ Gratitude.

Introduction

It is no wonder that we humans struggle to keep our spiritual side balanced in this very intense and busy world around us. With the fast-paced nature of modern life, it is challenging to prioritise our spiritual needs and still find time for practices that promote inner peace and well-being. The demands of work, family, and social life often leave little space for introspection and personal growth, leading many of us to feel disconnected from our spiritual side and ourselves. Modern life can be hectic, with long work hours, un-relenting constant deadlines, and endless to-do lists, leaving little time for us to devote to spiritual practices and deliberation.

Examples of the relentless modern world are all around us. Technological advancements have seen the rapid pace of technological innovation and change transform the way we work, communicate, and live our daily lives. Don't we all deal with the constant stream of social media, where we are constantly bombarded with notifications and alerts, leaving little room for quiet reflection.

Globalisation has meant the interconnectedness of the world economy and the rapid movement of goods, services, and people across borders have created highly competitive and fast-paced business environments. Environmental phenomena have left the planet facing various environmental challenges such as climate change, pollution, deforestation, and loss of biodiversity. These require urgent action to mitigate. Social unrest has highlighted societal issues such as inequality, political polarisation, and rising nationalism creating a climate of social and political unrest in many parts of the world.

Our work-life balance has left many people struggling to balance the demands of work with their personal and family responsibilities, leading to stress and burnout. These are just a few examples of the fast-paced modern world around us, which highlight the need for us to adapt and navigate these challenges in a thoughtful and contemplative way.

With the increasing demands of work, family, and social obligations, many of us struggle to find even a moment of peace or quiet in our daily lives. The long work hours that are often required in today's economy often leave us feeling drained and exhausted at the end of the day, leaving little time or energy for spiritual practices. Many of us even find ourselves caught in a cycle of work, sleep, and repeat, leaving no space for introspection or personal growth.

Some people are so busy that they see it as: sleep, wake up, and survive! This often leads to us feeling deluged, leaving little opportunity for self-reflection or contemplation.

The main challenge is that many people in modern times often find themselves struggling with life's challenges while also trying to hold on to their faith in God. This often leads not having a direct and meaningful spiritual connection with God, leaving us feeling unsupported and lacking guidance. However, we all know it is essential to find ways to incorporate spiritual practices into our daily life, even amidst the hustle and bustle of the modern world, to promote personal growth, well-being, and inner peace. However, finding time for prayer, meditation, mindfulness, and/or reading scriptures can be challenging in our fast-paced modern world.

That is where this book comes in. This book is all about a trusted and accepted method for us to re-connect with our God, in a very short space of time and effort, in this fast-paced world. It is important to recognize that God's love and support is always accessible to us, and we can initiate a deeper connection with Him by using the ancient Hawaiian tradition of Ho'oponopono. By understanding and employing the Ho'oponopono mantra, we can more easily re-establish our connection with God at any moment of the day, no matter the hour or minute.

Of course, this is all about the *re-connection*, until we can find the time and energy to properly settle down and spend more time in prayer, reading the Bible or fellowship. Over the next few pages, we will consider how to carry out the Ho'oponopono within our daily lives, and what it will mean to us going forward. However, before we get into the detail of what Ho'oponopono is, it is important for us to understand first why it is important to re-connect to our Saviour.

Why we should *want* to connect to God

The reasons for connecting to God can vary greatly depending on an individual's beliefs and situations in life. Some people may want to connect to God as a way to find inner peace and guidance in their lives, while others may need to connect to God to feel a sense of community and belonging. Still, others may connect to God to understand and make sense of the world around them, or to find comfort and solace in times of hardship.

Connecting to God can also provide a sense of hope and inspiration, and can offer individuals a sense of purpose and meaning in life. For many people, connecting to God can be a source of strength and comfort during difficult times, and can provide a sense of security and protection. Additionally, connecting to God can be a way to deepen one's spirituality and to develop a closer relationship with the Higher Power. Ultimately, the reasons for connecting to God are deeply personal, vary greatly from person to person and can be influenced by a wide range of factors, including one's upbringing, experiences, and spiritual journey.

Another reason may be that we are naturally sinners and we do keep on sinning, especially in the modern age. We know we can never say that we never make mistakes, +or that we have never sinned. It is therefore critical for us to accept our sinful nature and then to work to cleanse it.

For all have sinned and fall short of the glory of God

(Romans 3:23 NKJ)

The statement here is short and to the point: Everyone sins, everyone has sinned.

Some people may seek to reconnect with God to deepen their faith and commitment to their religious beliefs, while others may seek to reconnect with God to overcome personal challenges or to find a renewed sense of purpose in their lives. Some people may also seek to reconnect with God to gain a deeper understanding of the Divine and their place in the world. Ultimately, the aim of reconnecting with God is a deeply personal and spiritual journey that can be influenced by a wide range of factors, including one's experiences, beliefs, and relationship with God. Even years back, Pierre de Chardin (1959) expressed his contemplative inputs:

"To lose oneself in the Unfathomable, to plunge into the Inexhaustible, to find peace in the Incorruptible...To give one's deepest to Him whose depth has no end"

He implies that by connecting with God, one can find a sense of completeness and fulfilment that cannot be found elsewhere. Pierre further suggests that connecting with God can bring a sense of peace, understanding, and meaning to our life and, additionally can gain a deeper understanding of oneself and the world around us.

Let us look at some of the cognitive and practical reasons why we should *want* to connect to God.

Practical and Cognitive reasons

God is our Foundation

God serves as the foundation for our beliefs, values, and overall way of life, providing us with essential support, guidance, and comfort on a daily basis. By making God our foundation, we can access a reliable source of moral guidance and direction, which helps us remain true to our beliefs and ourselves.

In practical terms, relying on God as our foundation means that we draw strength and support from His higher power as we navigate the complexities of life. Connecting with God is thus an essential aspect of leading a fulfilling and meaningful life, as it provides us with a sense of purpose, direction, and stability amidst life's challenges.

He is the Rock; His work is perfect.
(Deuteronomy 32:4)

Jesus is the foundation of our salvation, and our hope and strength come from our relationship with Him. He is the one who gives us the strength and courage to face the challenges of life and to overcome sin and temptation.

By placing our faith and trust in Jesus, we are building our lives on a solid foundation that cannot be shaken. We can be confident that He will never leave us or forsake us. He will always be with us; guiding and leading us on the path of righteousness.

God keeps us grounded

Being grounded typically refers to a state of mental and emotional stability, where an individual is able to maintain a sense of balance and control even in challenging situations. Being grounded also refers specifically to the ability to remain composed and connected to one's inner self, even when faced with uncertainty or chaos.

Staying grounded requires maintaining a balance of emotional and mental stability, being in tune with one's innermost feelings, staying present in the moment, recognising one's self-worth, having a clear sense of purpose, connecting with nature, trusting oneself, and creating space for mindfulness. Overall, being and feeling grounded enhances our overall well-being, helping us to manage stress, improve relationships, and achieve our goals. Reconnecting with Jesus frequently and intimately can bring about a sense of balance, clarity, and coherence.

Sense of purpose

Discovering a sense of purpose is vital to finding fulfilment and meaning in life, and re-connecting with God is one way to achieve this. Knowing our purpose gives us a sense of direction and motivation, providing us with a reason to wake up each day and pursue our goals. Connecting with God also offers us a deeper understanding of our place in the world, and helps us identify our unique talents and abilities. Without this connection, we may struggle to find our purpose, leading to feelings of aimlessness, despair, and hopelessness. Therefore, it is crucial to re-connect with God to experience a sense of purpose and fulfilment in life.

He guides us into all truth; He will tell us things to come.
(John 16:13 NIV)
One of the key roles of the Holy Spirit is to guide us into all truth, helping us to understand the truth about God, the world around us and our place within it.

The Holy Spirit also reveals things to come, which means He gives us insight into the future and prepares us for what is to come. By listening to His voice and obeying His promptings, we can experience the fullness of the abundant life that God has planned for us.

Spiritual growth

Re-connecting with God not only gives us a sense of purpose and fulfilment but also provides an avenue for spiritual growth and development.

As we deepen our connection with the Divine, we can begin to explore our beliefs, values and innermost thoughts and feelings, leading to a greater understanding of ourselves and our connection to the world. Through this process of self-reflection, we experience transformation and develop a deeper understanding of our purpose and place in the world. Connecting with God also allows us to deepen our understanding of the world around us. The teachings and insights provided by God offer us a greater appreciation for the interconnectedness of all things and a more profound understanding of the natural world.

By exploring these teachings, we can experience spiritual growth and development, leading to a more fulfilling and meaningful life.

Moral guidance

Connecting with Jesus not only provides us with a sense of purpose and spiritual growth but also offers us clear moral guidance.

By connecting with Jesus, we gain access to His beliefs, values, and principles, which helps us to make decisions that align with our own beliefs and values. The teachings of Jesus offer guidance on a wide range of moral issues, such as compassion, forgiveness, honesty, and justice. By exploring and applying these teachings to our own lives, we can gain a deeper understanding of what it means to live a moral and ethical life. In addition, connecting with God also holds us accountable for our actions. The teachings of the Bible and other traditions teach us that we are responsible for our actions and will be held accountable for them in the afterlife.

Overall, connecting with God provides us with a sense of moral guidance that helps us to make decisions that align with our beliefs and values.

Provision and protection

God's provision and protection are essential aspects of His nature and character. As the creator of the universe, God is in control of all things and has the power to provide for us in ways of which we may not even be aware.

He provides for our physical needs, such as food, shelter, and clothing, as well as our emotional and spiritual needs, such as love, comfort, and guidance. When we trust in God, we can be rest assured that He will provide for us in ways that are best for us, even if we do not always understand how or when it will happen.

God is also our protector who watches over us and shields us from harm. He is aware of the dangers that we face in this world and can guide us to safety when we are in trouble. God's protection is not just limited to physical harm but also includes protection from spiritual harm, such as temptation and deception. When we follow God's guidance, we can avoid the dangers that may otherwise harm us. God's provision and protection offer us comfort and security in the knowledge that He is watching over us and caring for us. By trusting in God, we can experience His love and protection in our daily lives, which can help us to live with peace and confidence.

We *need* spiritual contentment

Spiritual contentment is a deeply personal and subjective experience that involves feeling a sense of inner harmony, satisfaction, and fulfilment. This state of being is characterised by a feeling of peace, serenity, and joy that comes from the recognition of the higher power of God who is the primary source of spiritual contentment.

Spiritual contentment also provides us with a sense of meaning and purpose in our lives. Through prayer, for instance, we can express our gratitude, ask for guidance and protection, and deepen our relationship with God. Spiritual contentment is essential for our overall well-being, as it can help us to feel more grounded, centered, and resilient in the face of life's challenges. It allows us to approach difficult situations with a greater sense of peace and equanimity, helping us to maintain our composure and avoid becoming overwhelmed by stress or anxiety. Moreover, spiritual contentment provides us with a sense of purpose and meaning, which can help us to navigate life's ups and downs with greater resilience and optimism.

> *"The inner presence of God, brought to us by the Spirit, is meant to transform us, while the charisms enable us to help others be transformed"* (Francis MacNutt, 2006:212)

Knowing God builds courage, faith and strength

As we gain knowledge and understanding of God, we often experience an increase in courage, faith, and strength. This is because we begin to recognise that God is the source of power, guidance, and support. By re-connecting with God, individuals can tap into this power and receive the strength and courage they need to face challenges in life.

By relying on God, we can find comfort and strength in difficult times. We can trust that God is our provider and protector, and that He will guide us through any challenges that we may face. This knowledge can help us remain resilient in the face of adversity, and can give us hope for the future. Ultimately, by recognising our connection to God, we can find the courage and strength to live a life that aligns with our values and beliefs. We can find joy in the journey of life, even in the midst of difficult times, knowing that we are not alone and that God is always with us.

Only by knowing God, can we know how to live

By understanding and connecting with God, we can gain a deeper understanding of our self and the world around us. Through our relationship with God, we can find a sense of purpose, meaning, and direction that helps us navigate the complexities of life. The Bible provides a wealth of wisdom and insight into how to live a good life, with teachings that promote kindness, compassion, forgiveness, and justice.

Living in God's ways means to strive to live a life guided by principles of love and compassion. By practicing these principles, we can find greater peace, joy, and fulfilment in our lives. Re-connecting with God provides a sense of accountability for our actions, as we believe that we will be held accountable for our choices in the afterlife. Only by cultivating a relationship with God and living in accordance with His teachings, will we live a fulfilling and meaningful life.

> *You will seek me and find me when you seek me with all your heart* (Jeremiah 29:13)

Seeking Jesus with all our hearts involves a sincere desire to know Him, to follow Him, and to obey His commands. When we seek Jesus in this way, we will experience the joy of His presence, the peace that comes from knowing Him, and the guidance and direction we need for our lives. We can be confident that Jesus is always near to us, ready to guide and direct us as we seek to follow Him.

A personal intimate relationship with the living God

As we get to know God more, the more personal an intimate relationship we will have with the living God. Deepening our relationship with God can be a transformative experience. As we continue to learn more about God through reading and studying scripture, prayer, attending church services, and engaging in other spiritual practices, we develop a stronger sense of connection with God. This connection can bring a sense of comfort, guidance, and support, which can help us to navigate life's challenges with greater ease and resilience. We begin to understand that God is a personal and loving being who cares for us deeply, and we can see how God's hand is at work in our lives.

Through this deepening of our relationship with God, we may also begin to experience a sense of closeness and intimacy that is unlike anything we have experienced before. This intimacy can bring a sense of peace and contentment, and it can help us to feel more grounded and centered in our daily lives. We may also find that we can develop a greater sense of empathy and compassion for others, as we begin to see them through the lens of God's love and grace. As our relationship with God becomes more personal and intimate, we may find that we are able to hear God's voice more clearly, and that we are better able to discern God's will for our lives. This can bring a sense of clarity and purpose to our lives, as we begin to understand more fully the unique path that God has set before us.

We may also find that we can live with greater integrity and authenticity, as we strive to live our lives in a way that reflects our deepening relationship with God. Our personal relationship with God can be a life-changing experience that brings a sense of peace, contentment, and purpose to our lives. By re-connecting with God, we can gain a deeper understanding of our self and the world around us, and we can live our lives in a way that is guided by love, grace, and compassion.

We *need* Salvation

Salvation, the act of being saved or redeemed, brings a sense of peace, fulfilment, and satisfaction. It implies that salvation is not just about being saved from eternal punishment, but it also brings an inner sense of well-being and contentment.

This idea is central to Christianity, where salvation is offered through faith in Jesus Christ. By accepting Jesus as our personal saviour, we are saved from eternal punishment and have eternal life with God. Salvation is also being re-connected and reconciled with God, and because of that reconciliation, our lives are transformed, and we experience inner peace, joy, and fulfilment. Salvation is a personal and intimate relationship with God, through which we experience a sense of contentment and peace.

> *Let your conversation be without covetousness; and be content with such things as ye have: for he hath said, I will never leave thee, nor forsake thee. So that we may boldly say, The Lord is my helper, and I will not fear what man shall do unto me.* (Hebrews 13:5-6)

Our confidence and hope come from our faith in God and His promises. We can trust that He is with us always and that He will never leave us or forsake us. We can face challenges with courage and confidence, knowing that God is on our side and that He will provide for our every need.

The best news is, as we get to know and understand God more and more, creation/life opens to us. As our understanding and knowledge of God deepens, we begin to see the world in a new light, and we are able to appreciate the intricacies, complexities, and interconnectedness of all things. We start to recognise the beauty of the natural world, the intricacy of its design, and the harmony that exists within it. As we come to understand more about God's character and His love for us, we begin to see our place in the world and our own being in a new way. We start to recognise the value and purpose of our existence and the unique gifts and talents that we have been given.

Through our re-connection with Jesus, we gain a sense of clarity, wisdom, and understanding about life. We begin to see the world through a different lens, one that is not clouded by our limited human perspective. This new perspective helps us to make better decisions, to find meaning and purpose in our lives, and to develop a deeper appreciation for the world and the Creator. As we come to understand

Jesus more deeply, we develop a sense of reverence and gratitude for the world and the Creator. We begin to see the beauty and purpose in all things, and we appreciate the gift of life more fully. We start to recognise the interconnectedness of all things, and we realise that we are all part of something much bigger than we are.

This sense of interconnectedness leads to a deep sense of responsibility to care for the world and to use our gifts and talents to make a positive difference in the lives of others.

We should know Him

God encourages us to seek a deeper understanding and relationship with Him and by re-connecting and developing a personal relationship, we can come to understand His nature, character, and will more clearly.

As we become more familiar with God's teachings and values, we gain a greater sense of purpose and direction in life. This can then help us to make better choices and decisions that align with our true values and goals. By seeking to know God more intimately, we can tap into His power and wisdom, which can help us overcome obstacles and achieve our full potential. Knowing God also helps us to develop a sense of inner peace and security, even in the face of life's challenges. This is because we trust in God's love, protection, and guidance. As we continue to deepen our relationship with God, we also become more compassionate, empathetic, and forgiving towards others, reflecting God's own love and kindness.

Ultimately, by knowing God, we can lead a fulfilling life that is grounded in spiritual principles and dedicated to serving others.

Our connection with God is what makes us Christian

Christian faith is built on the premise that our relationship with God is the foundation of our beliefs and practices. This relationship is achieved through faith in Jesus Christ, the son of God, and the Holy Spirit, which empowers us to live according to God's will. By accepting Jesus Christ as our saviour, we become part of the family of God and can begin to develop a personal and intimate relationship with Him. This relationship is characterised by prayer, worship, and reading of scripture, which allows us to gain a deeper understanding of God's character and will. Through this relationship, we can grow in our faith and become more like Christ.

The personal relationship with God that we cultivate as Christians is not just a set of rules or practices to follow, but a way of life that is centered on our love for God and others. We are called to love one another as Christ loves us, to be kind and compassionate to others, and to serve those in need. This way of life is only possible through our connection to God, which provides us with the strength, wisdom, and guidance we need to follow Christ's example. In essence, having a connection to God is what sets Christians apart from other belief systems. It is what gives us purpose and meaning in life, and it is what allows us to live a life of love, compassion, and service to others. Our connection to God is the foundation of our faith, and without it, we cannot truly call ourselves Christians.

I came that they might have life, and might have it abundantly. (John 10:10)

Through our relationship with Jesus Christ, we experience the abundant life that He promises, experiencing a deep and abiding sense of peace, joy, and purpose, knowing that we are loved by God and that He has a plan and a purpose for our lives.

What the Bible says about connecting to God

> *Do not be anxious about anything, but in every situation, by prayer and petition, with thanksgiving, present your requests to God.* (Philippians 4:6 NIV)
>
> Anxiety is a natural human response to stress and uncertainty, but we are called to take their concerns to God in prayer and trust that He will provide for their needs.

This is only possible as we abide in Christ and He in us. Philippians 4:6 teaches us to trust in God, bring our concerns to Him in prayer, be thankful, and approach Him with the right attitude. By doing so, we can experience peace that surpasses understanding, even in the midst of difficult circumstances.

> *I am the vine; you are the branches. If you remain in me and I in you, you will bear much fruit; apart from me you can do nothing.* (John 15:5 NIV)
>
> This verse from John 15:5 is a powerful reminder that our strength comes from being connected to Jesus Christ. As the vine nourishes and provides sustenance to the branches, we too must remain connected to Christ in order to produce good fruit in our lives.

It is only through our union with Christ that we can be truly fruitful and productive. Without Him, we are powerless and unable to accomplish anything of lasting value. This is because our human efforts are limited by our own strength and abilities, which are always fallible and imperfect.

When we remain connected to Christ and rely on His strength, however, we are able to bear much fruit. This fruit may come in the form of good works, spiritual growth, and a deepening relationship with God. Whatever form it takes, it is always a result of our union with Christ and our willingness to let His Spirit work through us. Let us remember that our strength comes from God alone. Let us seek to remain connected to Him and to rely on His Spirit to guide us and lead us in all things. And let us be encouraged by the promise that when we abide in Christ, we will bear much fruit and bring glory to His name.

> ***Consequently, faith comes from hearing the message, and the message is heard through the word about Christ.***
> *(Romans 10:17 NIV)*
> The message of the Gospel is profound in its simplicity; it declares the great news of God's love and mercy towards us through the death and resurrection of Jesus Christ.

It is through hearing this message that faith is born in our hearts, and we are given the opportunity to respond in repentance and belief. This verse from Romans 10:17 reminds us that faith comes from hearing the message about Christ. It is through the proclamation of the Gospel that people are brought to faith, as the Holy Spirit uses the preaching of the Word to convict and transform hearts. As we hear the message of the Gospel, we are confronted with the reality of our own sinfulness and our need for a Saviour.

We are shown the depth of God's love for us and the lengths to which He was willing to go to reconcile us to Himself. As we respond in faith to this message, we are given the gift of salvation, being forgiven of our sins and made new in Christ. We are clothed in His righteousness, adopted into His family, and given the promise of eternal life. May we never tire of hearing the message of the Gospel and may we always be eager to share it with others, that they too may come to faith and receive the gift of salvation. And may we be continually reminded of the truth that faith comes from hearing, and hearing through the Word of Christ.

> **By this we know that we abide in Him, and He in us, because He has given us of His Spirit.** *(1 John 4:13 NKJV)*
>
> This verse from reminds us of the incredible gift that we have been given as believers in Christ - the gift of the Holy Spirit. It is through the indwelling of the Spirit in our hearts that we are able to know and experience the presence of God in our lives.

The presence of the Spirit in our lives is not just a subjective feeling or emotion, but it is an objective reality that confirms our union with Christ. It is through the Spirit that we can bear witness to the reality of our faith, as the Spirit testifies to our hearts that we are indeed children of God. As believers, we have been given this incredible privilege of being indwelt by the Spirit of God. It is through the Spirit that we can live a life that is pleasing to God, as we are empowered and strengthened by His presence in our lives.

As we live out our faith in the world, we can bear witness to the reality of God's love and goodness through the way that we live and love others. We become living testimonies of God's grace and mercy, as we allow the Spirit to work through us and transform us into the likeness of Christ. May we never take for granted the incredible gift of the Holy Spirit in our lives, and may we always seek to live in a way that brings honour and glory to God, bearing witness to His goodness and love through our words and actions.

> **I will walk among you and be your God, and you will be my people.** *(Leviticus 26:11-12 NIV)*
>
> This verse reminds us of God's desire to be in relationship with us, to walk among us and to be our God. This is a beautiful promise that speaks to the heart of God's desire to be intimately involved in our lives.

God created us for relationship with Himself, and it is only through a deep and meaningful relationship with Him that we can truly experience the fullness of life. It is in God that we find purpose, meaning, and fulfilment, as He leads us on a journey of discovery and growth. As we choose to walk with God, we are given the opportunity to experience life in all its fullness.

We are given the gift of eternal life, as we are welcomed into God's family and given a place in His kingdom. This promise from God is a reminder that we are not alone, that we have a God who loves us and cares for us deeply. He desires to walk with us through the ups and downs of life, to guide us, to comfort us, and to be our constant source of strength and support. May we always remember that we have been given the incredible privilege of knowing and walking with God. And may we choose to embrace this gift fully, living our lives in a way that reflects the beauty of His love and the richness of His grace.

> ***Yes, a person is a fool to store up earthly wealth but not have a rich relationship with God.*** *(Luke 12:21 NLT)*
>
> This verse reminds us that our relationship with God is far more important than any earthly possessions or wealth we may accumulate.

While it is important to be responsible with the resources that God has given us, we must never allow our pursuit of wealth to overshadow our pursuit of a deeper relationship with Him. God desires for us to have a rich and meaningful relationship with Him, one that is marked by love, trust, and obedience. It is through this relationship that we are able to find true fulfilment and purpose in life, as we are transformed by His grace and empowered to live for His glory.

At the same time, God warns us about the dangers of allowing our pursuit of wealth to become an idol in our lives. He knows that the pursuit of earthly riches can easily become a trap, leading us away from Him and causing us to lose sight of what is truly important in life. As followers of Christ, we must always keep our priorities in order, seeking first the Kingdom of God and His righteousness, and trusting that all our earthly needs will be provided for as we put our faith and trust in Him. May we never lose sight of the incredible gift of relationship that God offers us, and may we always remember that true wealth and abundance can only be found in Him.

Come near to God and he will come near to you
(James 4:8 NIV)
This verse from James reminds us that our relationship with God is not one-sided. Rather, it is a two-way relationship that requires effort and intentionality on our part.

God wants us to draw near to Him, to seek Him with all our hearts, and to desire a deeper connection with Him. And when we take those steps towards Him, He promises to respond by drawing near to us in return. God is always accessible to those who seek Him, and He longs for us to come closer to Him. He desires to reveal Himself to us in new and powerful ways, to guide us through the challenges of life, and to fill us with His love and grace. But we must take the first step.

We must come near to Him, seeking Him with all our hearts and minds. We must make time for Him in our busy lives, seeking His presence through prayer, worship, and the study of His Word. As we do so, we will experience the truth of this verse first hand, as God draws near to us, filling us with His peace, His love, and His joy.
May we always remember that God is waiting for us, ready to draw near to us as we draw near to Him.

The Lord is near to all who call on him, to all who call on him in truth. *(Psalm 145:18 NIV)*

This verse from Psalm 145:18 is a powerful reminder of God's constant presence in our lives. It assures us that no matter what we are going through, God is never too far away and is always willing to help us when we call upon Him.

However, the verse also emphasises the importance of calling upon God in truth. This means that we must approach God with honesty and sincerity, laying our hearts bare before Him and seeking His help with humility and faith.

When we come to God in this way, we open ourselves up to His presence and power, and we allow Him to work in our lives in ways that we never could on our own. We experience the peace that comes from knowing that we are never alone, and we find the strength to face even the most difficult challenges with hope and courage. So let us take comfort in this verse and remember that the Lord is near to all who call upon Him in truth. May we always seek His help with sincerity and faith, knowing that He is always ready and willing to answer our prayers and guide us on our journey through life.

> **Let us draw near to God with a sincere heart and with the full assurance that faith brings, having our hearts sprinkled to cleanse us from a guilty conscience and having our bodies washed with pure water.** *(Hebrews 10:22 NIV)*

Drawing near to God with a sincere heart, full of faith, and free from a guilty conscience is the key to building and sustaining a strong relationship with Him.

Confessing our sins to Him and seeking His forgiveness is the first step in this process of purification. It is only through His cleansing that we can approach Him with confidence and assurance, knowing that we are forgiven and made new in Christ. The washing of our bodies with pure water also symbolises the need to purify our outward behaviour and conduct, aligning it with God's will and purpose for our lives.

> ***But as for me, it is good to be near God***
> *(Psalm 73:28 NIV)*
> Yes, when we draw near to God, we not only experience His goodness and love for ourselves but also become witnesses of His power and grace to others.

As we deepen our relationship with Him, we gain a greater understanding of His character and His plans for us, and we are better equipped to share that knowledge with others. We become living testimonies of God's transformative power and can inspire others to seek Him and draw near to Him as well.

> ***Seek the Lord while he may be found; call on him while he is near.*** *(Isaiah 55:6 NIV)*
> Seeking the Lord while He may be found and calling on Him while He is near is the best decision one can make. It leads to a life of purpose, meaning, and joy, and provides us with the guidance and wisdom we need to navigate through the challenges of life.

When we draw close to God, we also have the assurance that He is with us always, no matter what we may face. This is a great comfort and encouragement in times of difficulty and it gives us hope for the future. Therefore, let us seek the Lord with all our hearts and call on Him at all times, for He is always near to those who seek Him.

> ***Whoever conceals their sins does not prosper, but the one who confesses and renounces them finds mercy.***
> *(Proverbs 28:13 NIV)*
> Confessing our sins and repenting of them is essential in our relationship with God. It allows us to acknowledge our mistakes, take responsibility for them, and seek God's forgiveness.

When we confess our sins to God, we are being honest and transparent with Him, which is necessary for a healthy and genuine relationship. Additionally, confessing our sins can help us grow in our spiritual lives, as it enables us to learn from our mistakes and make changes that align with God's will for our lives.

> *If my people who are called by my name humble themselves, and pray and seek my face, and turn from their wicked ways, then I will hear from heaven and will forgive their sin and heal their land.* (2 Chronicles 7:14 NIV)

The verse teaches us that if we humble ourselves, pray, seek God's face, and turn from our wicked ways, then God will forgive our sins and heal our land.

It is a call to repentance and a reminder that God is always ready to forgive and restore those who come to Him with a sincere heart.

> *The Lord is near to all who call upon him, who call upon him in truth.* (Psalm 145:18 NIV)

This Psalm reminds us that God is near to all who call upon Him in truth.

This encourages us to seek God sincerely and honestly, knowing that He is always there to listen to our prayers and respond to them. It also emphasises the importance of having a personal relationship with God through prayer and worship.

> *Jesus answered, I am the way and the truth and the life. No one comes to the Father except through me.* (John 14:6 NIV)

This verse from the Gospel of John emphasises that Jesus is the only way to have a personal relationship with God and to receive eternal life. The verse underscores the importance of accepting Jesus as our Lord and Saviour and following His teachings to experience the fullness of God's love and blessings.

All these verses above tell us the same and one thing: a relationship with God is unlike any other relationship we may have. It is a deeply personal and spiritual connection that can bring about significant changes in our lives. When we invite God into our lives and allow Him to guide us, we can experience a sense of peace, purpose, and direction that we may not have had before. This does not mean that we will not face challenges or difficult times, but it does mean that we will have the assurance that God is with us and will help us through those times. As we grow in our relationship with Him, we can also experience growth in our character and values, leading to a more fulfilling and meaningful life.

The importance of sustaining a connection with our God

Connecting with God provides guidance and direction

A connection with God provides guidance and direction in life. Developing and nurturing a connection with God is crucial to finding guidance and direction in life.

We can achieve this connection through various means, such as prayer, reading of scripture, and acts of worship. As we connect with God and seek His guidance and direction, we become better equipped to navigate the challenges and difficulties that life throws our way. A more constant or sustained connection with God is important for our spiritual growth and development. As we connect with God, we deepen our understanding of who He is and what He desires for our lives. We come to understand His nature, character, and will, and this enables us to live in accordance with His plans and purposes for us.

As we develop our relationship with God, we become more attuned to His voice and guidance. We learn to recognise His promptings and leading, and we grow in our ability to discern His will for our lives. This helps us to make wiser decisions and to take action with greater confidence and clarity. Connecting with God also provides us with a sense of peace and comfort. As we turn to Him for guidance and direction, we can trust that He is with us every step of the way. This brings a sense of assurance and confidence, even in the midst of uncertainty and difficulty.

Our connection with God is essential for finding guidance and direction in life. By re-connecting with Him more often and more effectively, we deepen our understanding of who He is and what He desires for us, and we become better equipped to navigate life's challenges with confidence and purpose.

Connecting with God purifies the Soul

Connecting with God is an essential aspect of leading a virtuous and righteous life. Through regular practices such as confession, repentance, and the reception of sacraments, we can purify our souls and become more spiritually mature. Our connection to God helps us to grow in faith and to deepen our understanding of His nature and character. We learn to live in accordance with His will and become more compassionate and caring individuals. The more we RE-connect with God, the more we become inclined to serve others and do good deeds. This is because we are filled with a sense of love and compassion that comes from our relationship with Him.

Through prayer, reading of scripture, and acts of worship, we can develop a deeper connection with God, which in turn helps us to become more virtuous and righteous.

As Jesus said, in order to bear spiritual fruit and to grow in faith, we must remain connected to Him and live in Him. Our connection to Jesus helps us to develop a more intimate relationship with Him and to become more Christ-like in our thoughts and actions. Reconnecting with God helps us to purify our souls, become more virtuous and righteous, and develop a deeper understanding of His nature and character. Through our connection with Him, we become more inclined to serve others and to do good deeds.

Our relationship with Jesus is the foundation of our faith and helps us to bear spiritual fruit and grow in our faith.

> *Abide in me, and I in you. As the branch cannot bear fruit by itself, unless it abides in the vine, neither can you, unless you abide in me.* (John 15:4)

When we abide in Christ, we are connected to the source of all life and goodness. We receive strength, guidance, and wisdom from Him, and He produces fruit in us that brings glory to God. We cannot produce this fruit on our own, but only through our dependence on Him.

Abiding in Christ is a daily practice of surrendering our will and desires to Him and seeking His will and guidance in all things. It requires a humble and teachable heart, a willingness to trust and obey Him, and a commitment to remain in close relationship with Him.

Our connection to God leads to *more* in life.

Our connection to God is not just about following a set of rules or performing religious rituals. It is about having a personal relationship with the Creator of the universe. This relationship provides us with a greater sense of purpose and meaning in life, as we come to understand God's will and purpose for us. As we come to know God more intimately, our perspective on life changes, and we begin to see the world in a different way. We become aware of the beauty and interconnectedness of all things, and we appreciate life more deeply.

Our connection with God also leads to a sense of peace and contentment, knowing that we are not alone and that there is a purpose for our existence. By connecting and living in accordance with God's will, we can experience a more fulfilling life, we can make better decisions and navigate life's challenges with greater ease, knowing that we have the support and guidance of God.

We are also able to cultivate virtues such as compassion, kindness, and love, which enrich our lives and those around us. Our connection to God not only provides us with a sense of purpose and meaning, but it also gives us the strength and courage to face adversity. By knowing that we are not alone, and that God is always with us, we can face difficult situations with confidence and hope. Our connection to God provides us with a more fulfilling life, a sense of purpose and meaning, and the strength and courage to face adversity.

By seeking God's guidance and living in accordance with His will, we can experience the abundance of life that God intended for us.

Reconnecting strengthens our Faith

Knowing that the Lord is good, that He is on our side, and that He is always at work, even when we cannot see it, is what it is to have faith in Him. Having faith in God requires a personal connection with Him. We must know and understand who God is and what the Bible says about Him in order to have confidence in Him.

Faith in God is not simply a belief in His existence, but a trust in His love, wisdom, and power. This trust is built through a journey of continual growth and learning, as we deepen our understanding of God and His ways. Reconnecting with God is essential for strengthening our faith. When we understand that God is good, on our side, and always at work, even when we cannot see it, we develop a deeper confidence in Him.

Our own understanding of the existence of God and a life-altering trust in His truths is required for true faith. As we continue to connect with God through prayer, reading the Bible, and worship, we grow in our understanding of His nature and character. This growth leads to a stronger and more fulfilling faith, which helps us to face the challenges of life with courage and confidence.

Eternal life is only possible through a connection with God

Eternal life is not just an unending existence, but it is also the opportunity to live in the presence of God, and to experience eternal joy, peace, and fulfilment, for eternity. The only way to attain eternal life is by forming a connection with God. Having a personal and intimate relationship with God through Jesus Christ is the key to securing eternal life after death. As we continue to deepen our faith and connect with God, we experience a profound understanding of His nature and character. This intimate relationship with God brings about inner peace, joy, and satisfaction in our lives. We can also rejoice in the assurance of eternal life in the next world.

This knowledge that we are secure in our relationship with God and have the promise of an eternal life brings immense comfort and hope to our lives. Therefore, reconnecting with God is crucial as it grants us the most precious gift of eternal life.

Connecting with God focuses our mind and thoughts

When we truly connect with God, we can focus solely on our relationship with Him.
When we intentionally seek out moments of solitude with God, we create space for Him to speak to us and for us to hear His voice more clearly. This can lead to a deeper understanding of God's character, His will, and His ways. By focusing solely on our relationship with God, we

are able to strengthen our connection with Him and develop a more intimate relationship with Him. This can bring about a greater sense of trust and reliance on God, as we learn to surrender our worries and concerns to Him.

In doing so, we are better equipped to navigate the challenges and pressures of life, and to live in a way that is more aligned with God's will. Ultimately, by quieting our minds and hearts and focusing on our connection with God, we can experience a greater sense of peace, joy, and fulfilment in our lives. We can find solace in the knowledge that we are not alone. God is always with us, guiding us towards a deeper understanding of His love and grace.

> ### *And behold, I am always with you, to the end of the age*
> *(Matthew 28:20)*
>
> The Holy Spirit is the presence of God within us, guiding us, empowering us, and comforting us in all circumstances. Jesus' promise to be with us always gives us great assurance and confidence in our faith. No matter what challenges or trials we may face, we can trust that He is with us, empowering us to fulfil His purposes.

The Bible teaches us that our purpose in life is to love and serve God, and to bring Him glory in all that we do. This can be achieved by living a life that reflects the character of God, by sharing the good news of the Gospel with others, and by using our gifts and talents to honour God and advance His kingdom.

Ultimately, we find our true fulfilment and purpose in life when we are in a loving and obedient relationship with our Creator.

What is Ho'oponopono ?

The word Ho'oponopono (pronounced HO-oh-Po-no-Po-no) is derived from the Hawaiian language and is composed of two words: *ho'opono*, which means "to make right, *and pono*, which means rightness or correctness. The repetition of the word *pono*, in Ho'oponopono is significant because it emphasises the importance of making things right both within oneself and with others. In ancient Hawaiian culture, it was believed that when someone violated a spiritual law or committed an offense, it could lead to illness, misfortune, or other negative consequences.

Ho'oponopono was developed as a way to address these offenses and restore harmony and balance within the community. The practice involves a process of confession, forgiveness, and reconciliation, with the goal of resolving conflicts and healing relationships. It is typically facilitated by a trained practitioner or elder, but can also be done individually or within a family or community setting. The emphasis is on taking responsibility for one's actions and seeking forgiveness, rather than blaming or punishing others.

Traditionally Ho'oponopono is used primarily to resolve interpersonal and family conflicts and to clear negative energies from people and places. Examples of this these conflicts could include:

- **Interpersonal disagreements:** When two or more people were in conflict, Ho'oponopono could be used to help them understand each other's perspectives and find a way to reconcile.
- **Family feuds:** When families were in conflict, Ho'oponopono could be used to bring them together and resolve their differences.
- **Curses and negative energies:** Ho'oponopono could be used to address the effects of curses or negative energies that were believed to be causing illness or other problems.
- **Land conflicts:** When there had been battles or other conflicts on the land, Ho'oponopono could be used to clear the negative energies and restore balance and harmony.

In all of these scenarios, the focus of Ho'oponopono was on restoring balance and harmony, and on recognising the interconnectedness of all things. The goal was to heal relationships and restore a sense of peace and well-being to individuals, families, and communities.

Hawaiian psychology has long recognised the interconnectedness of the three minds of humankind: the conscious mind (*uhane*), the unconscious mind (*unihipili*), and the higher conscious mind (*aumakua*). These three minds are believed to be interconnected through *Mana*, the life-sustaining force of living creatures.

The concept of the three minds in Hawaiian psychology predates modern Western psychology's understanding of the conscious and unconscious minds. The *unihipili* is similar to what Western psychology would consider the subconscious mind, but it is also believed to have a personality and will of its own. The *aumakua*, or higher conscious mind, is considered the divine aspect of the self and is connected to the ancestors and spiritual realm. The interconnection between the three minds is believed to be facilitated through *Mana*, which is transmitted through the *unihipili* and can be accessed directly by the conscious mind.

Practices such as meditation can be used to alter consciousness and achieve this interconnection, allowing individuals to become aware of their innermost energies and clear them through the healing practice of Ho'oponopono. The logic is that by connecting our three sections of the mind, we become aware of our innermost residual energies, which can then be cleared up by the healing practice of Ho'oponopono.

To be able to do so, several cognitive factors contribute to the effectiveness of Ho'oponopono:

- Acknowledging that God is our Redeemer
- Understanding and accepting that everyone and everything is interconnected
- Open and honest communication, by all parties, is paramount
- We need to own up to our sins and transgressions, by accepting complete responsibility for our actions and experiences, instead of blaming others for causing pain
- Responsibility kick-starts the healing process and helps us move on from past negative experiences
- Forgiveness is critical for life to move forward, by recognising the interconnectedness of all beings with God, and the value that we can add to each other's lives through forgiveness and reconciliation

- Undergoing introspection to identify and release negative emotions, paving the way for personal growth and positive change

Ho'oponopono is therefore a process of addressing and healing conflicts within families or groups by acknowledging and taking responsibility for one's actions and their impact on others. It involves a process of repentance, forgiveness, and mutual restitution to restore harmony and balance within relationships and the community.

The Ho'oponopono intervention process can vary in some aspects depending on the cultural context or community where it is practiced, and generally involves:

- A community Senior/Leader is appointed to manage the process (known as Haku)
- Attendees gather in one room/area
- Meeting is opened with a prayer to our Creator
- Haku identifies the general problem
- Haku facilitates a fair discussion, where all get the chance to present their case (including sharing their feelings)
- Haku arranges transgressor/s to confess & victim/s to accept (participants are required to confess and ask forgiveness of each of the other participants)
- Haku arranges the 'cutting/severing the cord' (unravels entanglement that binds the offender and victim)
- Haku provides a summary
- Meeting is closed with a prayer
- Communal meal is attended by all

Remember, the ultimate goal is to restore balance and harmony within the community, and in turn, with God.

In recent years, Ho'oponopono has gained further popularity. It all started when Dr Ihaleakala Hew Len was a staff psychologist at Hawaii State Hospital and he worked with patients who had been diagnosed as criminally insane. Dr Hew Len's approach to Ho'oponopono focuses on taking personal responsibility for one's experiences and using the power of forgiveness and love to heal one's self and others. He believed that everything in the universe is connected and that negative experiences are a reflection of one's own thoughts, beliefs, and actions.

Dr Len's work with the criminally insane patients at the Hawaii State Hospital is often cited as a remarkable example of the effectiveness of his approach. According to legend, he was able to cure an entire ward of patients without ever physically seeing them or using traditional therapy methods. Instead, he would study their charts and then focus on clearing his own negative thoughts and beliefs in order to heal them. As he improved himself, the patients improved, and eventually, they were all released and the unit was closed. His philosophy was: to heal oneself or others, one must focus on clearing negative thoughts and beliefs and replacing them with positive ones:

> *"Your world is a reflection of you, so when you change, others change; and when others change, the world changes. So, when there's movement and change within you, there's no doubt that sooner or later, there'll somehow be a change somewhere out in the world."* (Len, 2017)

Len's approach to responsibility suggests that everything in our external reality is a projection of our internal reality. By taking responsibility for our internal reality, we can heal our self and others and create positive change in the world around us - the essence of the Ho'oponopono practice.

After Dr. Len's work with Ho'oponopono and the success he had with his patients at the Hawaii State Hospital, he went on to collaborate with bestselling author and self-help expert, Joe Vitale. Together they co-authored the book, *Zero Limits: The Secret Hawaiian System for Wealth, Health, Peace, and More*, first published in 2007. The book introduced Ho'oponopono to a wider audience, and it became a popular self-help and healing technique. It outlines Dr. Len's approach to healing and well-being through taking 100% responsibility and the practice of Ho'oponopono.

Vitale suggests that taking responsibility for our thoughts and actions can clear any negative thoughts or beliefs that may be causing problems in our lives. He explains that by doing this, we can achieve a state of inner peace and well-being, and this can have a positive impact on our external reality *"Ho'oponopono is simply a problem-solving process. But it's done entirely within yourself"* (Vitale, 2007:42).

However, the two approaches, self-help vs. God's word, are diametrically opposed. When we consider the self-help against the Ho'oponopono or Bible methodology, it is clear the difference in approach:

	Ho'oponopono	Self-help
Philosophy	We are sinners; if we repent to God, we will receive forgiveness	It is not our fault; bad experiences affect us and, if not taken care of, can hinder our future
I love you	God's love	Self-love
Forgive me	God wants us to accept responsibility	Forgive the self for harbouring negative thoughts, bad energies
Sorry	Expressing regret	Bad memories replay unpleasant scenarios
Thank You	Thanking God to receive His mercy	Thanking the self

The self-help industry often promotes the idea of personal autonomy and self-reliance, and while there is certainly value in taking responsibility for one's own life and choices, it is important to recognise that we are not self-made. We are shaped by our experiences, relationships, and environment, which is all ultimately dependent on God.

Self-help teachings that promote spiritual concepts or practices that contradict one's personal beliefs or values can obstruct spiritual growth and lead to confusion or doubt. As example, following self-help teachings that promote any new age spirituality or concepts that contradict scripture, such as the law of attraction, can impede our spiritual growth in Christ and can even lead us away from God. The bottom line is that if we live with the Spirit in our lives, the self-help world cannot compete with the God-help world.

Why, because as believers, we are guarded with the Word of God a source of guidance, comfort and wisdom. Being *guarded* by the Word of God refers to the fact that the teaching and guidance of the Bible helps us stay on the path of righteousness, and protects us from negative influences or temptations. The Word of God is the deep substance of our lives.

> *Put on the full armour of God, so that you can take your stand against the devil's schemes.* (Ephesians 6:11 NIV)
>
> Christians are engaged in a spiritual war, not only an earthly one. Using the armour of God is key to surviving this spiritual onslaught. We are called to speak out against evil (2 Corinthians 10:5), holding a firm defence against evil, allowing Christ to win the ultimate victory. Besides, what self-help promises will be lost at death; what God promises will last for all of eternity.

It is quite obvious that the Ho'oponopono process has undergone an evolution of sorts, originally a process of restoring balance and harmony within a family or community by acknowledging and addressing any issues or conflicts that were present, and linking to God for his guidance and blessing. Over time various adaptations of the Ho'oponopono process has emerged, including those that incorporate forgiveness and apologies as a means of healing relationships and promoting inner peace:

"The beauty of Ho'oponopono as a unifying force is that it adapts to your individual relationship with divinity whether that be ancient ancestral beings (as it was for the first Hawaiians who invented it), or the unspecified powers that be, the universe Yahweh, Allah or the Trinity. Being a Catholic, my understanding of Ho'oponopono is very strongly dependent on a Christian view of God" (Michelle Whitehouse, 2009).

Ultimately, the most important thing is that the process is approached with respect for its origins and intent, and that it is used in a way that promotes healing, harmony, and positive growth for all involved.

Reconnect to God with Ho'oponopono

Ho'oponopono is an ancient Hawaiian technique that promotes forgiveness and reconciliation. It requires individuals to acknowledge their actions and thoughts, and utilise affirmations and prayer to release negative energy, and establish equilibrium and accord. At the core of this process is a set of five phrases, which when repeated as a mantra, serve as powerful affirmations to initiate a re-connection to God:

- Adoration/Reverence (*I love you*)
    Adoration: acknowledging reverence for boundless perfection of God, with humility
    Reverence: displaying profound admiration and esteem towards God, characterised by a deep sense of respect and honour
- Supplication/Petition (*Please forgive me*)
    Supplication: making a sincere and earnest request or appeal, accompanied by a sense of humility.
    Petition: presenting a formal request or appeal to God, with the underlying belief in His goodness and benevolence to grant the request.
- Repentance/Atonement (*I am sorry*)
    Repentance: expressing genuine remorse and regret for our sins, and a genuine desire to turn away from them and make amends for any wrongs committed. This involves acknowledging the wrongdoing and striving to make positive changes in our behaviour and attitudes.

Atonement: making amends or reparations for our sins or wrongdoings, with the aim of restoring a harmonious relationship with Jesus Christ. It involves taking deliberate actions to reconcile with God and make things right.
- Thanksgiving/Gratitude (*Thank you*)
  Thanksgiving: expressing gratitude, joy, and relief for the blessings and good things that one has received from God. It involves recognising the goodness and generosity of God and acknowledging His provision and care, and offering thanks and praise in response.
  Gratitude: the expression of appreciation for the blessings and good things that God has provided, accompanied by a deep sense of pleasure, relief, and contentment.
- Wash away (*Clean, clean, clean*)
  Jesus Christ cleanses our sins and grants us forgiveness, though the shedding of his blood on the cross.
  Our sins are washed away and we are reconciled to God through our faith in Christ's redemptive crucifixion.
  Involves 'cutting the cord' from sin to soul (to be explained later)

In the following pages, we venture through the series of statements, which will then eventually make up the Ho'oponopono mantra.

Statement 1: "I love you" (Adoration/Reverence)

Adoration/Reverence - "I love you":

- Adoration - acknowledging and expressing reverence for the boundless perfection of God with humility
- Reverence - displaying profound admiration and esteem towards God, characterised by a deep sense of respect and honour.

This first step involves expressing our love and gratitude for our God, and is an important step in building a positive and meaningful relationship with Him. Starting off with the concept of love, we indicate our respect and admiration for Him, a good foundation for the rest of the message/mantra. Love is the foundation of all healthy relationships, including in our relationship with God. By expressing our love to God, we not only strengthen our relationship with Him but also cultivate a sense of inner peace and fulfilment within ourselves.

Love is not just an emotion but also a deeper recognition of our interconnectedness with all beings. Love is guided by compassion and understanding, which transcend the limitations of the individual ego. When we express love towards God, we become aware of the deeper, more essential aspects of our being and we recognise that our existence goes beyond the physical realm. We are connected to something greater than our self.

Expressing love towards God is also an acknowledgement of the spiritual or transcendent dimension of reality. It is recognition that there is more to life than what we can see, hear, touch, or taste. It is an acknowledgement that there is a higher power that governs the universe, and that we are a part of that power. By expressing love towards God, we affirm our connection to Him and open ourselves up to a deeper spiritual experience.

> *"In the prayer of adoration we love God for himself, for his very being, for his radiant joy"* (Douglas Van Steere, 1938:34)

The first step in the mantra, which involves expressing love and admiration towards God, is crucial in nurturing a positive relationship with Him. When we begin by expressing our love for God, we establish a connection with Him and open up a channel of communication, creating a reciprocal flow of energy, which allows us to receive His inspiration and guidance. Furthermore, expressing our love for God first off, sets the tone for our relationship and creates a foundation of trust and faith. It enables us to tap into our inner selves and intuition, and strengthens our belief in His love and guidance. By starting with this step we prioritise our relationship with God and recognise the importance of cultivating a deep connection with Him.

> **Though I can move mountains, without love I am nothing**
> (1 Corinthians 13;2)
> Through faith, we believe in the saving power of Jesus Christ, and we trust in Him for our salvation. However, it is through love that we demonstrate the reality of our faith to the world. We love because God first loved us, and our love for others reflects His love for us. As we wait for the Redeemer to come, we live out our faith by loving God and others.

Through our love, we can show the world the transforming power of the gospel and the reality of our hope in Christ. Ultimately, we will live with Christ in perfect love forever, free from all sin and pain.

From what we read in the Bible, if we have no love, we have nothing in life. For any relationship to grow and evolve, the first and most important ingredient is love. In fact, the essence of love is the presence of God in us, the source of love is God in us. True love comes from the grace of God. When we say *I love you God*, it is not just a verbal expression, but also a profound act of opening our hearts to the Him. This act of love involves numerous positive inputs and outputs that can have a transformative effect on our spirits. The words, and our deep feelings, clear all negative weight within our spirits, the words convert caught energies so they can flow again, allowing us to experience the miracle of the present moment.

Expressing love towards God is a way of acknowledging and honouring His presence in our life. It is a way of seeking comfort, guidance, or inspiration from Him. Expressing love towards God involves an act of gratitude and appreciation for the blessings and gifts that we have received. It is a way of recognising the beauty and wonder of the world around us, and the many ways in which He is present in our lives. Expressing love results in deepening our spiritual connection and relationship with Him, providing a source of comfort, inspiration and guidance, which facilitates a sense of peace, joy, and fulfilment in our life.

Expressing love helps to strengthen relationships and build trust. When expressing love towards God, it helps to deepen our faith and trust in Him, and provide a sense of peace and reassurance during difficult times.

Expressing love towards God is also an act of surrender, letting go of our own desires and trusting in a higher power to guide and direct our path. Expressing love towards God is a powerful way of strengthening our spiritual relationship and building trust in Him. It provides a sense of comfort, guidance, and support, and helps us to cultivate a deeper sense of faith and trust in Him.

> ***God is love; and He shall reign forever.*** *(Exodus 15:18)*
> When we allow God's love to fill us and overflow onto others, we become instruments of His love and light in the world. Through this, we participate in the eternal reign of love that God has established and experience the joy and peace that comes from being in a right relationship with Him.

Cultivating a relationship with God provides a sense of inner peace, well-being, and healing. When individuals express love towards God, they may experience a sense of connection to something larger than they may. This can provide a sense of perspective and help them to let go of worries and anxieties, leading to a greater sense of inner peace and calm. Expressing love towards God is acknowledging and releasing negative emotions, such as anger, frustration, or fear. By turning to Him for guidance and support, we are able to let go of negative feelings and find greater emotional balance and well-being.

> ***Enter his gates with thanksgiving and his courts with praise; give thanks to him and praise his name.*** *(Psalm 100:4 NIV)*
> Praise God that through faith we are His people and the sheep of His pasture. Instead of complaining, harbouring gratitude, and indulging in self-pity, we should count our blessings and praise the Lord for who He is and for His numerous gifts.

Let us enter His gates with thanksgiving and His courts with praise, and let us give thanks to Him and bless His name, for the Lord is good, His loving-kindness is everlasting, and His faithfulness endures throughout all generations.

When we cultivate a love for God, the love leads us to a deeper understanding of our purpose and meaning in life and inspires us to live according to our values and beliefs. For many believers, the love for God may mean a willingness to make sacrifices, whether it is giving up material possessions, dedicating time to prayer or religious practices, or prioritising service to others. These sacrifices are often seen as a way to live in accordance with their beliefs and also honour and show devotion to Him and.

At the same time, the love for God can also inspire individuals to prioritise their own happiness and well-being. By recognising Him within ourselves and acknowledging our own worth and value, we may feel empowered to make choices that support our physical, emotional, and spiritual health. Ultimately, the love for God inspires our faith, and prioritises our well-being and happiness. In other words, our re-connection provides a sense of purpose and direction, and lead to a greater sense of fulfilment and meaning in life.

> ***And thou shalt love the Lord thy God with all thine heart,***
> ***and with all thy soul, and with all thy might.***
> (Deuteronomy 6:5)
> As we grow in our relationship with God, our love for Him should deepen and become more Christ-like. This involves surrendering our own desires and will to God and allowing His love to transform us from the inside out. Through this process our love for God becomes more genuine and authentic.

Expressing love to God through words such as *I love you God,* is also a way to build a strong and lasting relationship with God. When we express our love to God, we are acknowledging our connection to Him and opening ourselves up to a deeper spiritual relationship. By saying these words, we are expressing our gratitude for the blessings in our lives, acknowledging the presence of God in our daily lives, and seeking a deeper connection to the Divine.

A strong and lasting relationship with God can provide a sense of comfort, guidance, and support throughout life's challenges and can help us to live in accordance with our values and beliefs. By expressing our love to God, we are making a commitment to our spiritual growth and development and inviting Him into our lives in a meaningful way.

In addition, saying *I love you God*, can also be an expression of our trust and faith in God. We may express our love for God as a way of affirming our belief in the power of divine love and guidance, and as a way of seeking comfort and support during difficult times. Overall, saying *I love you God*, is a way of recognising and appreciating the unique qualities and characteristics of God, and affirming our commitment to a deeper spiritual relationship with the Divine.

> ***And now these three remain: faith, hope and love. But the greatest of these is love.*** *(1 Corinthians 13:13)*
>
> While faith gives us a firm foundation in God's promises, and hope gives us the strength to persevere through trials and challenges, love is the greatest of them all. Love is the very nature of God, and as we love Him and love others, we become more like Him. Ultimately, love is what will remain even in eternity, as we experience the boundless love of God in heaven.

The love of God is all encompassing and boundless, reaching every person on this vast earth. As we continue to walk in God's love, our hearts become filled with love, expanding to receive even more of His divine love. Love takes hold of our hearts and permeates every aspect of our being, transforming us from the inside out. It is through experiencing and embracing God's love that we can truly come to understand our own worth and value as individuals. This love has the power to heal our deepest wounds and brokenness, providing us with the strength and courage to face life's challenges with renewed hope and purpose.

The love of God is an infinite and everlasting force that encompasses all of humanity. Surrendering ourselves to this love fills us with the fullness of God, and as we continue to walk in His love, our hearts expand to receive even more of His love. It is through experiencing and embracing God's love that we can discover our true worth and find healing and purpose in our lives.

> *"This is the perfect love about which the Apostle John wrote but it is beyond all I dreamed of. In it is personality. This love thinks, wills, talks with me, corrects me, instructs and teaches me.' And then I knew that God the Holy Ghost was in this love, and that this love was God, for ' God is love '. Oh, the rapture mingled with reverential, holy fear- for it is a rapturous, yet divinely fearful thing to be indwelt by the Holy Ghost, to be a temple of the Living God !"* (Samuel Brengle, 1954:7-8)

Beginning the mantra/prayer by saying **"I love you Lord God"** is initiating and expressing our love and devotion to God, with trust and faith, imbuing our desire to build a deeper, stronger and lasting relationship with Him.

The Ho'oponopono mantra:

"I love you" - commitment
"Please forgive me" - responsibility
"I am so sorry" - regret
"Thank you" - gratitude
"Clean, clean, clean" - purification

Statement 2: "Please forgive me" (Supplication/Petition)

Supplication/Petition - "Please forgive me":

- Supplication - making a sincere and earnest request or appeal for something, accompanied by a sense of humility.
- Petition - presenting a formal request or appeal to God, with the underlying belief in His goodness and benevolence to grant the request.

This second step involves asking for forgiveness from God for any harm that we may have caused: "Repentance is an inner change of mind resulting in an outward turning back, or turning around; to face and to move in a completely new direction" (Derek Prince, 2023).

Asking for forgiveness and showing repentance is an important step in the Ho'oponopono mantra. Repentance involves taking responsibility for our actions, acknowledging any harm or wrongdoing that we may have caused, and expressing genuine remorse for our behaviour. When we say "Please forgive me," we are recognising our own fallibility and imperfection, and seeking to make amends for any harm that we may have caused.

This may involve expressing regret for specific actions or words, or simply acknowledging our own limitations and seeking divine guidance and support. It is important to note that asking for forgiveness is not just about seeking absolution for our own actions, but also about seeking to repair and restore our relationship with God. It involves a willingness to learn from our mistakes, to make amends where possible, and to strive for greater compassion, kindness, and understanding in our relationships with others and with God.

> ***If we confess our sins, he is faithful and just and will forgive us our sins and purify us from all unrighteousness.*** *(1 John 1:9)*
>
> It is important to acknowledge and take responsibility for our sins and to turn away from them, seeking God's forgiveness and grace. No matter how great our sins may be, God's love and mercy are even greater, and through repentance and confession, we can be restored to a right relationship with Him.

When we say, *Please forgive me,* it typically means that we are acknowledging to have done something that has caused harm or wrongdoing and that we are asking for forgiveness and repentance from God. It involves acknowledging our mistakes and taking responsibility for our actions, particularly if we have caused harm or wrongdoing. It demonstrates our willingness to make amends and seek forgiveness from God for any actions that may have been hurtful or harmful.

Asking for forgiveness from God is an important aspect of many spiritual practices and is often seen as a necessary step in the process of repentance and spiritual growth. It involves a willingness to acknowledge our faults and shortcomings, and a commitment to learning from our mistakes and striving to do better in the future. By saying "Please forgive me" we are expressing our desire to be in the right relationship with God and to live in accordance with His will. It is our humble and sincere act of contrition that can help to foster a sense of inner peace and spiritual renewal.

Expressing remorse for the harm caused is an important part of seeking forgiveness from God. When we recognise that our actions have caused harm to God and/or His peoples, it is important to express genuine remorse and take responsibility for our actions. Expressing remorse involves acknowledging the pain and suffering that we have caused others, and showing empathy and compassion for those who have been affected by our actions. It also involves a commitment to making amends and taking steps to prevent similar harm from occurring in the future.

This step shows a willingness to take responsibility for our actions and make amends. It can help us to recognise the gravity of our actions and motivate us to take steps to prevent similar actions in the future. By expressing remorse, we can demonstrate our commitment to changing our behaviour and seek to repair the harm that has been done. By acknowledging our mistakes and expressing remorse, we demonstrate our willingness to learn from our mistakes and strive to be better people in the future. Ultimately, expressing remorse and seeking forgiveness from God is an important aspect of spiritual growth and development. It helps us to cultivate a greater sense of humility, compassion, and empathy, and to build stronger and more meaningful relationships with God and His peoples.

Offering to make amends or change our behaviour in the future is an important step in seeking forgiveness from God. It shows that we are taking responsibility for our actions and are committed to repairing the harm that has been done. It shows that we understand the impact of our actions and are willing to take steps to make things right. It also demonstrates our commitment to learning from our mistakes and growing as a person. By making a sincere effort to make amends, we can start to rebuild trust and repair relationships with others and with God.

Making amends can take many forms, such as apologising directly to the person or people we have wronged, taking actions to prevent similar harm in the future, or making reparations if possible. It is important to remember that making amends is not a way to avoid consequences or "make things right" automatically, but rather a way to show that we are taking responsibility and are committed to doing better in the future. This step can be challenging, but it is an important part of the process of seeking forgiveness and moving forward in a positive direction. Offering to make amends or change our behaviour in the future is an important step in seeking forgiveness from God and moving forward in our spiritual journey. It shows that we are willing to take action to repair the harm caused and demonstrate our commitment to living a life aligned with our values and beliefs. It can also be an opportunity for personal growth and learning from our mistakes.

> *"Whatever the character of your sin, confess it. If it is against God only, confess only to Him. If you have wronged or offended others, confess also to them, and the blessing of the Lord will rest upon you"* (Ellen White, 1890)

Showing humility and a willingness to learn from the situation is an important step in seeking forgiveness from God. It involves acknowledging that we do not have all the answers and that we are open to learning and growing from our mistakes. By showing humility, we are demonstrating a willingness to put aside our pride and ego and accept the guidance and wisdom that comes from a higher power. This can be a transformative experience that allows us to deepen our relationship with God and become more compassionate, empathetic, and understanding individuals.

Atonement is an important aspect of seeking forgiveness from God. It involves taking responsibility for our actions and making efforts to correct any harm that we may have caused, either through direct action or by doing good for others. Remember, forgiveness refers to the act of pardoning someone who has done wrong or has harmed us. It involves letting go of anger and resentment towards that person, and choosing not to hold their actions against them.

Atonement, on the other hand, refers to the act of making amends for wrongdoing or harm caused. It involves taking responsibility for one's actions and making efforts to repair the harm that has been done, either through direct action to undo the consequences of the act, equivalent action to do good for others, or some other expression of remorse. In short, forgiveness involves letting go of anger and resentment towards someone who has harmed us, while atonement involves taking responsibility for the harm caused and making efforts to repair it.

Forgiveness and repentance requires humility and a willingness to confront our own flaws and limitations. Admitting to wrongdoing and accepting responsibility for our actions is not an easy task, but it is necessary for personal growth and healing.

Through this process, we can learn from our mistakes and make positive changes in our lives.

Saying **"Please forgive me"** is initiating and expressing our regret and remorse, with trust and faith, imbuing our desire to build a deeper, stronger and lasting relationship with God. In effect, we are considering two aspects here:

- Firstly to say "Please forgive my sins against you" - involves our transgressions that we need to take personal responsibility for.
- The second aspect is "Please forgive me for doubting you" - we have not maintained faith that God will guide and protect us, and we have doubted His promises and potentials.

The Ho'oponopono mantra:

"I love you" - commitment
"Please forgive me" - responsibility
"I am so sorry" - regret
"Thank you" - gratitude
"Clean, clean, clean" - purification

Statement 3: "I am sorry" (Repentance/Atonement)

Contrition/Repentance/Atonement- "I am sorry":

- Repentance - expressing heartfelt remorse and regret for one's sins, and a genuine desire to turn away from them and make amends for any wrongs committed i.e. acknowledging the wrongdoing, seeking forgiveness, and striving to make positive changes in one's behaviour and attitudes.
- Atonement - making amends or reparations for one's sins or wrongdoings, with the aim of restoring a harmonious relationship with God.

Repent is from the Greek root word *metanoeō*. It does not mean to apologise, it means to acknowledge your way is wrong and God's way is right. It is a complete change in your view of the world. It means that I admit I am a sinner, and that I feel sorry for the fact I have sinned. However, true repentance, as it is defined, actually means a complete and total change of mind.

To repent is to not only feel sorry for my sin, or even just to confess it to God. To repent of my sin is to turn from it, and to turn towards Christ where we will be filled with the Holy Spirit. In fact, repentance is the first and only step to enter the Kingdom of God.

> ***Now repent of your sins and turn to God, so that your sins may be wiped away.*** *(Acts 3:19 NLT)*
>
> Repentance is a major theme in Jesus' ministry. In order to be saved, we must accept that our sins are wrong and that God provides the way we should live. We need to allow the belief to change us, inside and out.

We need to confess our sins, name them specifically, be accountable and be responsible for them.

I am sorry, is a phrase of apology in the form of remorse or regret. It is a way of acknowledging the wrong that has been done and seeking forgiveness from God, as well as a commitment to try to make amends for one's actions. It is important to note that simply saying *I am sorry God*, is not enough on its own. It should be accompanied by genuine remorse and a sincere effort to make things right, with taking responsibility for one's actions and making amends in the spiritual and physical world.

This means taking responsibility for one's actions, making amends with any individuals who may have been harmed by the wrongdoing, and making a commitment to avoid similar behaviour in the future. Overall, saying *I am sorry God*, can be an important part of the process of seeking forgiveness and making amends. It is important to take ownership and responsibility for our thoughts and actions when apologising, and express remorse for the harm or wrongdoing that was caused. It is also important to take steps to make things right, whether that means making amends or committing to change our behaviour in the future. Here are some key points to keep in mind when apologising:

> "The forgiveness of sin is promised to him who repents and believes" (Ellen White, 1890)

Take Ownership

Taking ownership of our actions means accepting responsibility for what we did or failed to do, without making excuses or blaming others. It is important to acknowledge that we were the one who caused the harm and accept the consequences of our actions. This can be difficult, especially if feeling ashamed or embarrassed, but it is an essential part of making a sincere apology. Here are some key points to keep in mind when taking ownership of our actions:

- Acknowledge our role: Start by admitting that we are responsible for what happened. Use "I" statements to take responsibility for our actions, such as "I'm sorry for what I did" or "I understand that my behaviour was hurtful."
- Be honest: It is important to be honest about what happened and why we acted the way we did.
- Be accountable: Accept the consequences of our actions, whether that means offering an apology, making amends, or facing disciplinary action. Being accountable shows that we understand the seriousness of the situation and are committed to making things right.
- Commit to change: Once we have taken ownership of our actions, commit to making changes to prevent similar incidents from happening in the future.

Taking ownership of our actions is a crucial step in making a sincere apology and repairing any damage to our relationship with God. It shows that we are willing to be accountable for our behaviour and committed to making things right.

Repent

> "Repentance means you change your way of thinking... this is possible for those who surrender to the grace of God. The renewed mind is the result of a surrendered heart"
> (Bill Johnson, 2003:37)

Express remorse: Apologise sincerely and have express genuine regret for the hurt or damage caused. When expressing remorse, it is important to be sincere and genuine in our apology. Our words should convey empathy and demonstrate that we have thought deeply about the situation and the impact of our actions. Some practicalities when expressing remorse:

- Take responsibility for our actions i.e. acknowledge our role in causing the hurt, and take full responsibility for our actions.
- Use "I" statements, say "I'm sorry for the hurt I caused you"
- Offer to make amends: If there is anything we can do to make things right, offer to do so.

By expressing remorse and apologising sincerely, we can demonstrate our willingness to take responsibility for our actions and make things right with God. This can help to repair the relationship and move forward in a positive way. When we make amends, we are taking concrete actions to make things right and demonstrate our commitment to making up for our mistake/s.

A genuine apology is often the first step in making amends, however, we need to follow through on your promises. Once we have made a commitment to make amends, it is important to follow through on our promises. This demonstrates our sincerity and commitment to repairing the harm caused/reconnecting to God.

By taking these steps to make amends, we can demonstrate our commitment to repairing the harm caused and rebuilding trust with Him. It may take time, but by showing that we are willing to take responsibility for our actions and make things right, we can begin to repair the relationship and move forward in a positive way.

> ***Repent therefore and be converted, that your sins may be blotted out, so that times of refreshing may come from the presence of the Lord.*** *(Acts 3:19 NIV)*
>
> *Repenting is not just an intellectual exercise; we need to allow the belief to change us, inside and out. That does not mean we will never sin again. The goal of repentance is not to become perfect but to develop a deep abhorrence for sin and a desire to live in obedience to God's will.*

Commit to Change

If our actions were the result of a pattern of behaviour, we need to commit to making changes to prevent similar incidents from happening in the future. We need to be specific about the steps we will take to address the root cause of the problem. Committing to change is a crucial part of making amends and repairing relationships after causing harm or damage. If our actions were the result of a pattern of behaviour, it is important to take steps to address the root cause of the problem and prevent similar incidents from happening in the future. Here are some tips for committing to change:

- Acknowledge the problem: The first step in committing to change is acknowledging the problem and taking responsibility for our actions. This means being honest with ourself and others about the behaviour that led to the harm or damage.

- Identify the root cause: Once we have acknowledged the problem, it is important to identify the root cause of the behaviour. This could involve reflecting on our past experiences and understanding what triggers the behaviour, or seeking help.
- Develop a plan for change: Based on our understanding of the root cause, develop a specific plan for change. This might involve setting boundaries, learning new coping mechanisms, or seeking support from the Bible or other like-minded individuals.
- Follow through on our plan: Making changes to our behaviour can be difficult, but it is important to follow through on our plan and demonstrate our commitment to change.

By committing to change and taking concrete steps to address the root cause of the problem, we can demonstrate our willingness to prevent similar incidents from happening in the future and rebuild trust with the other person or God. It may take time, but by showing that we are committed to making things right, we can begin to repair the relationship and move forward in a positive way.

> ***I can do all this through him who gives me strength.***
> *(Philippians 4:13)*
> Through the power of God's strength, we can overcome any obstacle and achieve all that He has called us to do. We must rely on His strength, wisdom, and guidance to accomplish His will in our lives.

Follow through

It is important to follow through on our commitments and take concrete steps to make things right. This will help rebuild trust and repair any damage to our relationship with God.

Following through on our commitments is a critical part of making amends and rebuilding trust after causing harm or damage to others. When we make commitments to repair the harm caused, it is important to take concrete steps to demonstrate our commitment to making things right. Here are some tips for following through:

- Take action: The first step in following through on our commitments is to take action. This means doing what we said we would do, and taking concrete steps to repair the harm caused.
- Be consistent: Consistency is vital when it comes to following through on our commitments. This means consistently showing up and taking action to repair the harm caused, even when it is difficult or inconvenient.
- Communicate regularly: Communication is important when it comes to following through on our commitments. Keep God informed about our progress, and let Him now if there are any challenges or obstacles we are facing.
- Be patient: Repairing relationships takes time, and it is important to be patient as we work to follow through on our commitments, so be prepared to demonstrate our commitment over time.
- Seek feedback: Finally, seek feedback from God, He will respond, if we allow Him !

By following through on our commitments and taking concrete steps to repair the harm caused, we can begin to rebuild trust and repair the relationship with our Creator. It may take time and effort, but by demonstrating our commitment and consistency, we can show that we are serious about making things right.

Remember, apologising is not easy, but it is an important part of taking responsibility for our actions and repairing the harm caused. It is important to remember that apologies can go a long way in healing relationships and resolving conflicts, and that taking full responsibility for one's actions and expressing genuine remorse is the key to a sincere and effective apology.

> *If we confess our sins, He is faithful and just to forgive us our sins and to cleanse us from all unrighteousness.*
> (1 John 1:9 NIV)

Confession should be a regular part of our prayer life, as we come before God with honesty and humility, laying our sins before Him and asking for His forgiveness. By confessing our sins daily, we can stay in right relationship with God and experience His love and grace in our lives. As we confess our sins and receive God's forgiveness, we are empowered to live a life of obedience and holiness, reflecting the character of Christ to the world around us.

Taking responsibility involves repentance, when we show that we are very sorry for something bad we have done in the past, and wish that we had not done it. Regretting sin and turning from it are related to repentance, but are not the precise meaning of the word. In the Bible, the word repent means "a change of mind that results in a change of action" (see Acts 26:20). Repentance requires a willingness to be honest with oneself about one's own shortcomings and failures, and to abandon any attempts to justify or excuse one's behaviour through self-righteousness or deceit. True repentance requires that we face our sins head-on, without excuses or justifications. It involves a deep humility and a willingness to accept responsibility for our actions, even when it is difficult and uncomfortable to do so. Only then can we experience the deep and lasting change that comes through true repentance. When we are willing to let go of our self-righteousness and deceit, and instead embrace the truth about ourselves, we can experience the freedom, joy, and peace that come through a genuine and sincere repentance.

> **Turn us back to You, O Lord, and we will be restored.**
> *(Lamentations 5:21 NKJV)*
> Only God has the power to bring about true restoration and renewal, we must turn back to Him in repentance and faith to experience His healing and grace.

The idea is that by confessing our sins, acknowledging them before God, and placing our faith in Jesus Christ, we will receive forgiveness for our sins. It is important to note that forgiveness is not automatic but is granted solely by God's grace. It is also important to understand that forgiveness does not necessarily mean that the consequences of our actions disappear, but it does at least mean that we are no longer separated from God by our sin.

> *"I warn you that if you want to continue to have the power of God manifested through you, you have to live in the Spirit continually; not occasionally, not once a day but always. Oh beloved, at any cost, pay any price to live in it, for it is worth the world"* (Smith Wigglesworth, 1940)

Saying **"I am sorry"** involves expressing ownership and responsibility for our thoughts and actions, and demonstrating remorse for the harm or wrongdoing that was caused, with trust and faith, imbuing our desire to build a deeper, stronger and lasting relationship with God.

In effect, we are considering two aspects here:

- Firstly to say "I am sorry, *for my sins and transgressions*" - transgressions against God which we need to take personal responsibility for.
- Secondly, saying "I am sorry, *for doubting you*" - where we have not maintained faith that God will guide and protect us, and we have doubted His promises of protection.

The Ho'oponopono mantra:

"I love you" - commitment
"Please forgive me" - responsibility
"I am so sorry" - regret
"Thank you" - gratitude
"Clean, clean, clean" - purification

Statement 4: "Thank you" (Thanksgiving/Gratitude)

Thanksgiving/Gratitude "Thank you":

- Thanksgiving: Expressing gratitude, joy, and relief for the blessings and good things that one has received from God. It involves recognising the goodness and generosity of God and acknowledging His provision and care, and offering thanks and praise in response.
- Gratitude: The expression of appreciation for the blessings and good things that God has provided, accompanied by a deep sense of pleasure, relief, and contentment.

This penultimate step involves expressing our thankfulness and gratitude for the opportunity to make amends and for the blessings in our life. This is an important step in the process of making amends and moving forward after wrongdoing. It is a way for us to show appreciation for the opportunity to make things right, and to acknowledge the blessings in our life. When expressing thankfulness and gratitude, it includes considerations such as:

- Being grateful for the support and guidance
- Reflecting on the positive things in life and expressing gratitude for them
- Showing appreciation for the lessons learned from the situation, an important step in personal growth and healing

The phrase "thank you" not only involves the words themselves but also the intention and attitude behind them. For example, if someone says "thank you" begrudgingly or insincerely, it may not carry the same weight or impact as someone who genuinely expresses gratitude with sincerity and appreciation. It is important not just to say "thank you" but also to genuinely mean it and express it with a positive attitude and sincere intention. When gratitude is expressed in this way, it not only makes us feel valued and appreciated, it can also create a positive impact on us by promoting positive emotions and fostering stronger relationships. When we take the time to thank God, we are recognising His value as Creator, and the role He plays in our lives.

This strengthens our connection with Him and creates a positive dynamic in our interactions. So, to convey true gratitude and appreciation, it is important to take a moment to reflect on the impact that Gods actions has on our lives and to express our sincere appreciation for His support. This can be done through words and actions. Ultimately, the key is to be genuine and heartfelt in our expression of gratitude, as this will make the biggest impact on the person we are thanking.

> ***Do not be anxious about anything, but in everything, by prayer and petition, with thanksgiving, present your requests to God. And the peace of God, which transcends all understanding, will guard your hearts and your minds in Christ Jesus.*** *(Philippians 4:6-7)*
>
> God says we should turn to Him in prayer and thanksgiving when we feel anxious or overwhelmed. By doing so, we can experience His peace, which is beyond our understanding and can guard our hearts and minds from worry and fear.

Expressing gratitude will also have numerous positive effects on our well-being and relationships with God, and with others. Research has shown that gratitude can increase happiness, reduce stress and anxiety, improve sleep, and even boost our immune system. When we feel appreciated and valued, we are more likely to continue helping others, and to feel motivated to make a positive impact in the world. This leads to stronger relationships, greater social support, and a sense of belonging and connection. Furthermore, expressing gratitude can also help us cultivate a more positive mind-set, by focusing on the good things in our lives, rather than dwelling on the negative. This can lead to greater resilience in the face of challenges, and a greater sense of overall well-being and satisfaction. Saying "thank you" is much more than just a simple phrase. It is a powerful tool for building connections, expressing gratitude, and improving our overall well-being. By taking the time to express our appreciation and gratitude towards God, we create a more positive, supportive, and fulfilling life for ourselves and everyone around us.

When considering our interpersonal relationship with God, saying "thank you" is our way of seeking absolution or release for any sins that may have occurred. By acknowledging our positive approach and expressing sincere appreciation, we show that we recognise and value Gods efforts. Additionally, expressing gratitude and saying "thank you" can also provide closure in situations where there may be lingering negative feelings or unresolved issues. By expressing appreciation and gratitude, we can let go of any negative emotions and move forward with a sense of resolution and peace. Expressing gratitude and appreciation can certainly have a positive impact on our relationships and sense of well-being, and can help to create a sense of closure and resolution in certain situations.

When considering Ho'oponopono, it is believed that by taking responsibility for our thoughts and actions, we can clear negative energy and restore balance and harmony in our lives, relationships, and the world around us. The practice involves repeating four phrases: *I'm sorry, Please forgive me, Thank you,* and *I love you,* as a way to express remorse, ask for forgiveness, express gratitude, and cultivate love and compassion. Furthermore, by repeating these phrases as a mantra, one can release negative thoughts and emotions that may be blocking the flow of positive energy.

Ho'oponopono is a powerful way to reconnect with God, self and others, it is a way to let go of negative thoughts and emotions and cultivate love and compassion. It can help to improve relationships and bring a sense of peace and harmony to our life. The Ho'oponopono practice is based on the belief that everything in the universe is connected and that negative thoughts and emotions can block the flow of positive energy. By taking personal responsibility for our thoughts and actions, we can clear this negative energy and restore balance and harmony with Jesus Christ.

> **When Jesus saw their faith, he said, 'Friend, your sins are forgiven.** (Luke 5: 20 NIV)
>
> Through His life, death, and resurrection, Jesus provides the way for humanity to be reconciled with God and to have eternal life. By accepting Him as our Lord and Saviour, we receive the gift of salvation and are empowered to live a new life; guided by the Holy Spirit.

Saying **Thank you,** involves expressing gratitude for the opportunity to learn from the situation and to invite God's healing energy into our lives, with trust and faith, imbuing our desire to build a deeper, stronger and lasting relationship with Him.

The Ho'oponopono mantra:

"I love you" - commitment
"Please forgive me" - responsibility
"I am so sorry" - regret
"Thank you" - gratitude
"Clean, clean, clean" - purification

Statement 5: "Clean, clean, clean" (Wash away, cut the cord)

- Wash away *Clean, clean, clean*
- Our sins are cleansed and washed away, and we are reconciled to God through faith.
- We remain sinners, and therefore need to constantly re-connect and *clean*.

The last phrase of "clean, clean, clean" is used as a final statement in the Ho'oponopono mantra, to reinforce the idea of cleansing and purification. By repeating the fifth phrase *clean, clean, clean*, after considering all the contents of the phrases, we are affirming our commitment to cleansing and purifying all aspects of the problem or situation. The *Clean, clean, clean* is the cutting and severing of the cord, the unravelling of entanglements that bind us to our sins and transgressions.

I love you is used to affirm one's commitment to love and compassion, and to invite positive energy and healing into one's life; "I'm sorry" is used to acknowledge responsibility for any negative thoughts, emotions, or actions that may have contributed to the problem.

Please forgive me is used to ask for forgiveness from God for any harm caused.

Thank you is used to express gratitude for the opportunity to learn from the situation and to invite healing energy into one's life. When repeating the words *clean, clean, clean,* we are cutting and severing the cord that bind us to our sins and transgressions, thereby affirming our re-commitment to Jesus Christ, inviting positive energy and healing into our relationship.

> ***Don't you know that you yourselves are God's temple and that God's Spirit lives in you ?*** *(1 Corinthians 3:16)*
>
> We can rely on the Holy Spirit to help us navigate through life and to grow in our relationship with God. The presence of the Holy Spirit within us helps us to discern truth and resist temptation, leading us to live a life that honours and glorifies God.

By repeating the words *clean, clean, clean*, we are affirming our commitment to letting go of negative energy and emotions, and inviting positive energy and healing into our life with God. By repeating the words while simultaneously using a *'hand swipe'* action (palm facing the body, swiping away from the body), we are also physically re-affirming our commitment to Jesus Christ. The physical act of the hand swipe away from the body symbolises the act of sweeping all the sins and pain away into the distance, and starting off fresh with a new clean slate.

Overall, the *clean, clean, clean*, is a simple yet powerful way to simulate, symbolically the washing way of our sins and transgressions, with faith in God's grace. This last phrase also provides a sense of "closure" (cutting the cord) to the process, a foot hold on the reconnection with God.

Saying **"Clean, clean, clean"** with a simultaneous hand swipe action (palm facing the body, swiping away from the body), reinforces the idea of cleansing and purifying our mind, body and spirit of negative thoughts and energy, with trust and faith in God's grace, imbuing our desire to build a deeper, stronger and lasting relationship with Jesus Christ.

In effect we are again considering further aspects here:

- Firstly, saying "Clean, clean, clean" reiterates the first four Ho'oponopono statements
- Secondly, saying "Clean, clean, clean" with a swish of the hand, provides a philosophical and physical means to 'wipe away our sins'
- Finally, saying "Clean, clean, clean" provides us with a mental closure (cutting the cord from our transgressions) in our reconnection to God

The Ho'oponopono mantra:

"I love you" - commitment
"Please forgive me" - responsibility
"I am so sorry" - regret
"Thank you" - gratitude
"Clean, clean, clean" - purification

Now that we have been through the basic logic behind the mantra, we will now have a read on how to use it in the initiation to re-connect to God.

How and when to use the Ho'oponopono statements/prayer practically ?

The way to say the Ho'oponopono prayer/mantra of *I'm sorry, Please forgive me, Thank you, I love you* and *Clean, clean, clean* can be personalised to your own preferences and the situation you find yourself in. Here are some practical thoughts you may want to consider:

- The Ho'oponopono mantra is a prayer designed to be simple and manageable, and is an effective method to 'focus' the mind.
- Although the words of each statement should remain the same, the statements can be verbalised in any order that feels right for us.
- The statements have tremendous power in that they contain the ever-important aspects of reconnection – the power of repentance, forgiveness and gratitude.
- While some individuals prefer a quiet and peaceful place to sit comfortably and free from distractions, others use the mantra instinctively and randomly throughout their day.
- Most individuals suggest they use one or two statements with clean clean clean, or even just one with clean clean clean, all depending on their thoughts and time available.
- Practitioners say that when verbalising the mantra out loud, the words leave a deeper impact on them as individuals.

The purpose of the prayer is to let go of negative emotions, thoughts and memories that are blocking the flow of love and healing in our life, and to restore our connection with Jesus Christ:

- Begin by saying *I love you,* to affirm your commitment to love and compassion, and to invite the holy Spirit's positive energy and healing into your life.
- Then *say Please forgive me*, and ask for forgiveness for any harm caused.
- Next say *I'm so sorry*, and reflect on any negative thoughts, emotions, or actions that may have contributed to your situation.
- Then say *Thank you*, and express gratitude for the opportunity to learn from the situation and to invite healing energy into your life.
- Then finally say *Clean, clean, clean*, to reinforce the idea of cleansing and purifying your relationship to God.

People have said there are various opportunities of where and when to find a few minutes to concentrate on the mantra:

- First thing after waking up, focusses the mind on our Lord.
- During the first lap of the pool of the early morning swim
- When towelling off after the morning shower
- When walking to catch the bus, while driving to work
- Periodically at work when we experience some of Gods beauty e.g. flowering plants in the building, birds on the windowsill
- While walking the dog
- Even when walking from one office to the next...the list goes on.

People also say they use the statements to refocus on the 'now', to get mindful of what are the priorities at the moment - to re-focus on God.

Remember, we can recite the mantra as often as we like, and the more we do so, the more we clear our spirit and reconnect with God.

The bottom line, using the Ho'oponopono prayer is quick and directed, thus can be used whenever time allows - the more we clean, the better ! When we recite the statements often, it becomes a habit, eventually our subconscious mind will take over and repeat these phrases for us almost continuously, therefore we end up praying (cleaning) virtually all day long.

The Ho'oponopono mantra:

"I love you" - commitment
"Please forgive me" - responsibility
"I am so sorry" - regret
"Thank you" - gratitude
"Clean, clean, clean" - purification

Our desire to re-connect with God should not be a once-off or weekly/monthly event, but a continuous reality every minute of our lives. It is a process. We must surrender ourselves to Him all the time, and all day we should choose to remain in his Spirit. We should want to keep on being filled with the Spirit, all the time.

Be filled with the Spirit (Ephesians 5:18)
The Holy Spirit is *the* source of power and wisdom through which we experience a deeper relationship with God and empowers us to live a life that honours Him.

God, the Creator, stands apart from His creation, marked by righteousness and holiness. His aim in creating us is to share in His inheritance and commune with us. However, our sinful nature has severed this connection, inherited from Adam. Despite our unworthiness, God redeems us through Jesus, who willingly bore the penalty of sin and validated His sacrifice through resurrection. Spiritual rebirth is necessary to grasp this, as salvation is received through faith in Jesus. Salvation isn't earned by deeds alone but received through faith and repentance. By embracing Jesus as Lord, we're justified and granted access to God's presence. This transformation, initiated by God's Spirit, brings righteousness and communion with Him.

To remind us, the practice of Ho'oponopono is based on the principles of Hawaiian spirituality and the belief in the interconnectedness of all things. Overall, the Ho'oponopono mantra is a useful and powerful tool for self-reflection, forgiveness and healing when used with intention, sincerity, and an open heart - an effective way for us to re-connect to God.

What to expect when Re-Connecting to God

When connecting to God through the Ho'oponopono mantra, there are many potential positive consequences:

A constant awareness of God's presence, with a deep sense of intimacy

This involves a journey of spiritual transformation and growth, where we become more like Christ and are able to live in harmony with God's will and purpose for our lives. By cultivating a constant awareness of God's presence and developing a deeper intimacy with Him, we can experience a profound sense of meaning and purpose in our lives.

Ho'oponopono practice can help individuals to achieve this by promoting self-reflection, forgiveness, and gratitude, all of which are essential components of a healthy spiritual life. Through this practice, we can learn to let go of negative emotions and beliefs that may be blocking our connection with God, and instead cultivate a spirit of love, compassion, and humility. Ultimately, this can lead to a transformation of the self, where we become more aligned with God's will and purpose for our lives, and can live more fulfilling and meaningful lives. Ho'oponopono helps in this journey by providing a framework for taking personal responsibility, releasing negative emotions, and cultivating love and compassion.

Through regular practice, the mantra facilitates our connection to God, improving our relationship with Him, simultaneously bringing physical and emotional healing, inner peace and harmony, and clarity of mind.

God, be merciful to me, the sinner! (Luke 18:13)

It is important to remember that repentance is not just about feeling sorry for past mistakes but also involves a conscious decision to turn away from sin and embrace a new way of life centered on God's love and grace.

As Christians, we are called to repent and turn to God regularly, not just once at the beginning of our faith journey. It is a continual process of seeking forgiveness and asking for God's help to live a life that honours Him.

Inner peace and harmony

The practice of the Ho'oponopono mantra is a powerful tool to help us tore-connect and re-focus, to cultivate inner peace and harmony in our lives. By taking personal responsibility for our thoughts and actions, we can become more aware of the negative patterns and behaviours that may be causing harm or blocking progress in our life. This awareness can lead to a deeper understanding of oneself and the world, and can help us to identify the root causes of our negative thoughts and emotions.

When we take personal responsibility for our thoughts and actions, we also take ownership of our own healing and growth process. This can empower us to make positive changes in our lives and to take steps towards achieving our goals and aspirations. Additionally, by taking personal responsibility for our thoughts and actions, we can also learn to forgive ourselves for past mistakes and to see our own humanity and imperfection. This self-forgiveness can lead to greater self-compassion and self-acceptance, which can further contribute to our inner peace and harmony.

It is important to note that taking personal responsibility for our thoughts and actions is not about blaming oneself or feeling guilty for past mistakes, but rather about recognising that we have the power to change and make better choices in the present and future. It is a process that requires self-awareness, humility, and a willingness to learn and grow.

> *"The inner presence of God, brought to us by the Spirit, is meant to transform us, while the charisms enable us to help others be transformed"* (Francis MacNutt, 2006:212)

Improved relationships

By expressing remorse, asking for forgiveness, and expressing gratitude and love, the mantra 'structure' helps to improve our relationships with God, and to bring about a greater sense of unity and connectedness. Taking personal responsibility for our thoughts and actions can also lead to improved relationships. By acknowledging and apologising for any harm caused, and taking steps to make things right, we can repair and strengthen our damaged relationship with God.

The Ho'oponopono structure focuses on forgiveness and reconciliation, which can help us to let go of grudges and resentment, and to heal and restore relationships that may have been impacted by past hurt or conflict. By taking responsibility and asking for forgiveness, we can also learn to communicate more effectively, to listen actively, and to empathise with others, and with God. This leads to greater understanding and compassion, and to more meaningful and fulfilling relationships. As we let go of negative thoughts and emotions, and cultivate love and compassion, we may also find that we connect more deeply with God and are able to build a more authentic and loving relationship with Him.

> ***I have come that they may have life, and have it to the full***
> (John 10:10)
> Jesus promises abundant and eternal life to all who follow Him, not just physical existence but a fullness of life that comes from knowing and being in a relationship with God.

Physical and emotional healing

The Ho'oponopono mantra promotes physical and emotional healing by clearing negative energy and restoring balance and harmony in the body and mind. The practice of forgiveness and reconciliation helps us to let go of grudges and resentment, which reduces stress and tension in the body, and promotes physical and emotional healing. The mantra also helps us to cultivate positive thoughts and emotions, such as love and compassion, which can have a positive impact on physical and emotional well-being.

Research has also shown that mindfulness and self-compassion practices, such as Ho'oponopono, can reduce stress, anxiety, and depression, and improve overall mental health.

Increased spiritual connection

By taking personal responsibility for our thoughts and actions, we can learn to identify and release negative thoughts and emotions that may be blocking our connection to the higher power. The letting go of grudges and resentment, will further reduce stress and tension in the body, and promote spiritual connection. The Ho'oponopono mantra also helps us to cultivate positive thoughts and emotions, such as love and compassion, which have a positive impact on spiritual well-being. By focusing on connecting to God, Ho'oponopono practice also helps us to find a sense of purpose and meaning in our lives, and to experience a deeper sense of connection to Him.

The main focus of the Ho'oponopono mantra is on personal responsibility, forgiveness and connecting with the higher power and inner self. By regularly engaging in the Ho'oponopono mantra, we can develop a closer relationship with God and gain deeper insights into the nature of truth and reality:

Greater clarity and purpose

Our connection to Jesus helps to provide a sense of direction and clarity in life, and to guide decision-making and actions.

Increased inner peace and happiness

Living in alignment with Jesus promotes a sense of inner peace, contentment, and happiness. By cultivating positive emotions such as love, gratitude, and compassion with Jesus, we experience a greater sense of well-being and fulfilment in life.

Spiritual growth and transformation

Employing the mantra often, facilitates spiritual growth and transformation by helping us to deepen our connection with God. This involves developing a greater sense of purpose, meaning and fulfilment in life. The Ho'oponopono mantra facilitates our life long journey of spiritual growth and transformation, leading us towards a deeper understanding to Jesus.

Experiencing Gods love

When using the Ho'oponopono mantra to re-connect to God, your feelings will stir and your heart will begin to warm. The more often you connect to God, the more you will enjoy the process and the more you will feel and experience the love in it all.

Clarity of mind

By taking personal responsibility for one's thoughts and actions, we learn to identify and release negative thoughts and emotions that may be clouding our mind and causing confusion. The Ho'oponopono mantra of repeating *I am sorry*, *Please forgive me*, *Thank you*, and *I love you*, is a way of expressing remorse, seeking forgiveness, and promoting healing. By engaging in this practice, we are able to cultivate a greater sense of self-awareness and understanding of our own thought patterns and emotional responses. As negative thoughts and emotions are released, we also experience a greater sense of inner peace and calmness, which can help to reduce stress and anxiety and promote mental clarity.

By focusing on connecting with God and inner self, Ho'oponopono practice can also help individuals to find a sense of purpose and meaning in their lives, and to experience a deeper sense of inner peace and harmony, which can lead to greater clarity in the mind.

Security and contentment

The Ho'oponopono mantra facilitates our access to Jesus who is the source of guidance and inspiration to us all. He is as the source of wisdom, comfort, and guidance for believers. By following His guidance, we feel a sense of security in knowing that we are living in accordance with God's will. This sense of security is accompanied by a deep contentment and satisfaction in our life. By aligning ourselves with God's will, we experience greater peace, fulfilment, and purpose in our lives.

> *"Intimacy is the main purpose of prayer. And it's through relationship that God entrusts to us the secrets of His heart, that we might express them in prayer"* (Bill Johnson, 2003:64)

Remaining re-connected to God

There are a few ways to stay connected with God through Ho'oponopono practice:

Practice regularly

Making Ho'oponopono prayer a regular habit is essential for maintaining a consistent connection with God. By setting aside time each day to engage in this practice, individuals can establish a routine that helps them stay focused and committed to their spiritual growth. One effective way to establish a regular practice is to set aside a specific time each day for Ho'oponopono practice. Many people find it helpful to practice first thing in the morning or before bed, as this can help to set the tone for the day or facilitate a peaceful transition into sleep.

When establishing a regular practice, it is important to be consistent and make a commitment to yourself to engage in the practice each day. This can be challenging at first, but with time and practice, it will become easier to integrate this habit into your daily routine. It is also important to create an environment conducive to your Ho'oponopono practice. This may involve finding a quiet and peaceful space where you can engage in the practice without distractions or interruptions.

It may even be helpful to keep a record of your Ho'oponopono practice, such as in a journal or diary. This can help you track your progress and reflect on your experiences, providing insight into your spiritual growth and development.

> *"Oh, this thing of keeping in constant touch with God, making him the object of my thought and the companion of my conversations, is the most amazing thing I ever ran across. It is working. I like God's presence so much that when for a half hour or so he slips out of mind, as he does many times a day, I feel as though I had deserted him, and as though I had lost something very precious in my life"*
> (Frank Laubach, 1950)

Create an Atmosphere to Hear from God

You may feel the need to create an atmosphere that is conducive to hearing from God. By atmosphere we mean the climate, environment, or predominant mood that surrounds us. Atmosphere is created by attitudes, and certain attitudes enhance or hinder our relationship with God. An atmosphere that is quiet, safe, positively energy-orientated, and loving facilitates connectivity.

> *"Our God is not made of stone. His heart is the most sensitive and tender of all. No act goes unnoticed, no matter how insignificant or small. A cup of cold water is enough to put tears in the eyes of God. Like the proud mother who is thrilled to receive a wilted bouquet of dandelions from her child, so God celebrates our feeble expressions of gratitude"*
> (Richard Foster, 1992:89-90)

Using the Ho'oponopono mantra sporadically throughout the day can also be an effective way to maintain a connection with God and cultivate positive thoughts and emotions. The mantra can be used as a tool to help individuals stay centered and focused on their spiritual growth throughout the day, even amidst the distractions and stresses of daily life. Finding opportunities to use the mantra throughout the day, such as during a break at work or while walking the dog helps us to stay connected to our spiritual practice and remain grounded in our daily lives.

These moments of concentrating on the mantra, help us to pause, reflect, and cultivate a sense of inner peace and calm. Using the mantra in this way can also help us to become more aware of our thoughts and emotions throughout the day, and to bring a greater sense of intentionality to our actions and interactions. For example, by using the mantra to cultivate positive thoughts and emotions, we can bring more love, compassion and forgiveness into our daily lives. This will have a positive impact on us and those around us.

Ultimately, whether practicing Ho'oponopono regularly or using the mantra sporadically throughout the day, the goal is to cultivate a deeper connection with God and to promote spiritual growth and well-being. The key is to find what works best for you and to make a commitment to incorporating this practice into your daily life in a way that feels authentic and meaningful.

Cultivate positive thoughts and emotions

As mentioned earlier, Ho'oponopono practice can help individuals to cultivate positive thoughts and emotions, such as love and compassion. When individuals focus on positive thoughts and emotions, they are more likely to attract positive experiences and outcomes into their lives. This is because thoughts and emotions are powerful energy forms that can shape our reality and influence the world around us. By focusing on positive thoughts and emotions, we strengthen our connection with God. This is because God is associated with the qualities of love, compassion, forgiveness, and grace.

Cultivating positive thoughts and emotions is an essential part of Ho'oponopono practice. By focusing on these qualities, individuals strengthen their connection with God, attract positive experiences and outcomes, and build deeper and more fulfilling relationships with others.

Fear not, for I am with you; be not dismayed, for I am your God; I will strengthen you, I will help you, I will uphold you with my righteous right hand.

(Isaiah 41:10)

No matter what challenges we may face in life, God is with us and will provide us with the strength and help that we need.

Practice forgiveness

Forgiveness is an integral part of Ho'oponopono practice. By letting go of grudges and resentments, individuals can clear their minds and hearts and make room for a deeper connection with God. Holding grudges and resentments can block our connection to God and prevent us from experiencing inner peace and well-being. When we hold onto anger, bitterness, and resentment towards others, we are essentially carrying negative energy within us.

This negative energy can manifest in various ways, such as physical and emotional tension, stress, anxiety, and depression. Moreover, holding onto negative emotions can create a cycle of negativity that can impact our relationships with others, our own well-being, and our ability to connect with God.

In Ho'oponopono practice, forgiveness is viewed to release these negative emotions and clear our minds and hearts of negativity. This practice involves acknowledging our own role in a situation and taking responsibility for our part in it. It also involves extending compassion and forgiveness to others, recognising that they too are imperfect and may have been acting from a place of pain or misunderstanding. By practicing forgiveness, we can let go of grudges and resentments, and make room for a deeper connection with God. This can lead to a greater sense of inner peace, joy, and well-being, as well as improved relationships with others.

Forgiveness is an integral part of Ho'oponopono practice, as it helps us to release negative emotions and clear our minds and hearts, making room for a deeper connection with God and promoting overall well-being.

> ***Trust in the Lord with all your heart and lean not on your own understanding; in all your ways submit to him, and he will make your paths straight.*** (Proverbs 3:5-6 NIV)
> As we trust in the Lord, submit to Him, and follow His lead, He will guide us on a path of righteousness, peace, and joy, and help us to fulfil His purposes for our lives.

Engage other forms of connection

Here are some examples of spiritual practices that Christians may use to draw near to God:

Reading the Bible and other Christian literature can help us gain a deeper understanding of God's character, will, and plan for our life. It can also provide inspiration, comfort, and guidance.

Regular prayer and Bible study help us deepen our relationship with God and understand His will for our life. Prayer is a form of communication with God that allows us to express their gratitude, ask for guidance, and share their hopes and dreams. Through prayer, we can develop a stronger sense of trust and faith in God, and cultivate a deeper sense of inner peace and well-being.

Christian meditation involves focusing our mind on God and His Word, allowing us to quiet our mind and re-connect with God on a deeper level. Through meditation, we can become more aware of our thoughts and emotions, and learn to observe them without judgment or attachment. This can help to reduce stress and anxiety, and promote feelings of calm and relaxation.

Incorporating prayer and meditation into our daily routine can help to strengthen our connection with God in several ways. First, it can help to quiet the mind and reduce distractions, allowing us to focus more fully on our spiritual practice. Second, it can help to cultivate a sense of inner peace and well-being, which can make it easier to connect with God on a deeper level. It may further help to develop a regular spiritual practice that becomes a part of our daily routine, making it easier to maintain a consistent connection with God over time.

Worshiping with other believers is an essential part of the Christian faith. Attending church regularly allows us to learn from and encourage other believers, participate in corporate worship, and receive teaching and guidance from pastors and leaders.

Listening to Christian media can provide encouragement, inspiration, and teaching from Christian leaders and teachers.

Serving others is an essential part of the Christian faith. When we serve others, we demonstrate God's love and compassion and fulfil Jesus' command to love our neighbour as yourself.

Whether we choose to pray, meditate, or both, it is important to find a practice that resonates with us and that we feel comfortable with. We can start with just a few minutes each day and gradually increase the amount of time as we become more comfortable with the practice. With regular practice, prayer and meditation can become powerful tools for cultivating a deeper connection with God through Ho'oponopono practice.

> ***But he who unites himself with the Lord is one with him in spirit.*** (1 Corinthians 6:17 NIV)
>
> Believers are not just followers of Christ, but are united with Him in a deep, spiritual sense. This unity brings believers into a close relationship with God, allowing them to experience the fullness of His love, grace, and power.

Take in the sights, sounds and smells of our surroundings

By being fully present and aware of our surroundings, we can experience a deeper sense of connection to the world around us. Here are some tips for practicing this:

- Use our senses: As we go about our day, try using all our senses to take in the surroundings. Notice the colours, shapes, and textures of the things around us. Listen to the sounds of nature, traffic, or people talking. Smell the scents of the environment, whether it is the smell of fresh flowers or the aroma of coffee brewing.
- Slow down: It's easy to get caught up in the hustle and bustle of daily life, but slowing down can help us to be more present in the moment. Take a few deep breaths and intentionally slow down the pace as we move through our day.
- Practice gratitude: As we take in the sights, sounds, and smells of your surroundings, take a moment to feel gratitude for the world around us. This can help us to appreciate the beauty, wonder of life, and feel more connected to our surroundings.
- Be curious: Approach the world around you with a sense of curiosity and wonder. Ask questions about the things you see, hear, and smell, and try to learn more about the world around you.

> ***Command those who are rich in this present world not to be arrogant nor to put their hope in wealth, which is so uncertain, but to put their hope in God, who richly provides us with everything for our enjoyment***
>
> *(I Timothy 6:17 NIV)*

God provides us with good things for our enjoyment, but he cautions against putting too much emphasis on material wealth and becoming arrogant or selfish as a result.

Practice gratitude

Expressing gratitude for the blessings in our lives can help individuals to cultivate a sense of appreciation and connection to God. By expressing gratitude for the blessings in our lives, we can cultivate a sense of appreciation and connection to God.

Here are some ways to practice gratitude in your daily life:

Keep a gratitude journal: Take a few minutes each day to write down things that you're grateful for. It can be as simple as a beautiful sunset or a delicious meal.

Focus on the positive aspects of your life can help shift your perspective and cultivate a sense of gratitude. Express gratitude to others: Take time to thank the people in your life who have made a positive impact on you. Write a thank-you note or simply express your gratitude in person. This can help you to feel more connected to others and strengthen your sense of community.

When facing challenges or difficult situations, it can be easy to focus on the negative. However, practicing gratitude during these times can help shift your perspective and provide a sense of comfort and hope. Look for the lessons or opportunities for growth in difficult situations, and express gratitude for them.

Gratitude affirmations are powerful tools for shifting your mind-set and cultivating positive emotions. Incorporate gratitude affirmations into your daily practice, such as *I am grateful for all the abundance in my life* or *I am thankful for the love and support of those around me*. By practicing gratitude regularly, you can cultivate a deeper connection to God and experience a greater sense of joy and fulfilment in your life.

By practicing these, we can cultivate a deeper sense of mindfulness and presence in our daily life, which can help us to connect more often and more deeply with God. It is important to remember that using the Ho'oponopono mantra takes practice and effort, and with a few repetitions, will flow more readily and easily.

The Ho'oponopono prayer:

"**I love you**" - commitment
"**Please forgive me**" - responsibility
"**I am so sorry**" - regret
"**Thank you**" - gratitude
"**Clean, clean, clean**" - purification

Going Forward

Take responsibility

Acknowledging and accepting that our actions or choices have led to a certain outcome, whether it is positive or negative. It involves being accountable for our thoughts and behaviours, and owning up to the consequences of those actions. In the Ho'oponopono mantra, taking responsibility is an important step in the forgiveness process as it allows us to reflect on our actions and take steps to make amends. Taking responsibility also means that we are willing to change and make a better choice in the future, an essential aspect of personal growth and development.

By taking responsibility, we can learn from our mistakes and make positive changes going forward. It also helps to build trust and respect in relationships, and is an important part of personal and professional growth. When we take responsibility for our actions and choices, we become empowered to make positive changes and create the life we want. It allows us to move away from a victim mentality and take charge of our circumstances.

Furthermore, taking responsibility is not just owning up to our mistakes, but also recognising our strengths and using them to make a positive impact. By taking responsibility for our actions, we build self-confidence and self-esteem, which are important for overall well-being. By acknowledging our part in creating a situation, we can release any feelings of guilt or shame and move towards a place of forgiveness and reconciliation. This practice of taking responsibility can lead to greater understanding and empathy towards God, and ourselves and ultimately help peaceful life and us to live a more fulfilling.

> ***Seek the LORD and his strength; seek his presence continually !*** (1 Chronicles 16:11)
> We should make seeking God a constant priority in our lives, not just something we do when we have a specific need or problem. By seeking God's presence continually, we open ourselves up to His guidance, His wisdom and His blessings.

Be open to the guidance, wisdom and messages that God communicates to us

This can involve being attentive to one's thoughts, feelings, and intuition, as well as being open to signs and symbols that may be present in the natural world or in everyday life. It also involves being willing to follow God's guidance, even if it may be difficult or uncomfortable. It is also important to note that listening to God may involve learning to discern His voice from other voices, such as one's own thoughts, the influence of others, or even deception. This can be done through developing a deeper relationship with God through Ho'oponopono, prayer, reading the Bible and other spiritual texts, studying the teachings of religious leaders, and seeking the guidance of spiritual mentors.

Additionally, being open and receptive to God's guidance may mean being open to change, to letting go of old ways of thinking and being, and to embracing new ways of living, which can be challenging but ultimately bring greater peace, fulfilment, and purpose to one's life.

By cultivating openness and receptivity to God's guidance, individuals can deepen their connection to God and live more fulfilling and purposeful lives. By being open to His guidance, we can gain a greater understanding of their purpose and direction in life. They can also gain a sense of peace and comfort in knowing that they are not alone and that God is always with them.

Being receptive to God's guidance can also help us to make better decisions, as we are able to discern what is truly important and aligned with our values and purpose. It can also help individuals to overcome challenges and obstacles that may arise in life, as they can draw strength and wisdom from their relationship with God. In addition, cultivating openness and receptivity to God's guidance can lead to a greater sense of gratitude and appreciation for the blessings in one's life.

By recognising the role that God plays in our life, and being open to His guidance, we can feel a deeper sense of connection to the world around us and a greater sense of purpose in our daily actions. Overall, by cultivating openness and receptivity to God's guidance, individuals can live more fulfilled and purposeful lives, with a deeper sense of connection to themselves, to others, and to God.

> "There is no mode of life in the world more pleasing and more full of delight than continual conversation with God"
> (Brother Lawrence, 1977)

Have passion in our endeavour

Having passion in one's endeavours is important because it provides energy, motivation, and drive. Passion can help one to overcome obstacles and challenges, and to persist in the face of adversity. It can also inspire creativity, innovation, and excellence. When one has passion in what they are doing, they are more likely to be fully engaged and invested in the process, which can lead to better outcomes and greater satisfaction.

Furthermore, having passion in what one is doing can also help to connect with a sense of purpose and fulfilment, which can be a vital component in connecting with God. It is important to note that having passion does not mean that the task will be easy, but it will give you the determination to overcome the obstacles and the motivation to achieve your goals. Passion is also linked with having a positive attitude, and this can be a powerful tool in connecting with God.

Showing passion can be done in a variety of ways, depending on the situation and the person:

- Speak with enthusiasm and energy
- Take initiative and take action towards our goals i.e. by putting in the effort and hard work required to achieve our objectives.
- Share our personal experiences and how our passion has impacted our life.
- Maintain a positive attitude and outlook, will also help to keep us motivated and engaged.
- Be true to ourselves and our passions.
- Consistently show our passion in our actions, words and behaviour.

Showing our passion can help to deepen our connection with God, as it can help to align our actions with our combined values and purpose. In terms of deepening one's connection with God, consistency in our passion can help to create a sense of purpose and meaning in our life, as it allows for a greater sense of alignment with God's will and purpose.

> *"We should not be satisfied with anything less than a close connection with Christ"* (Ellen White, 1890)

Freedom and salvation are offered to us, and we should grasp the precious promises of God by living faith. We should trust him as a child trusts his earthly parents. We should feel such love toward him that we cannot betray his confidence in us, or distrust him under any circumstances.

Have Faith

Having faith means having a belief in something greater than you, and trusting that everything will work out for the best. It involves having trust and confidence in a higher power, such as God, and in the goodness of the universe. It also means to trust in oneself and in one's abilities.

Having faith can help in connecting with God in a number of ways.

- Believing that everything happens for a reason and that a higher power is guiding us can help to alleviate anxiety and worry with a sense of peace and calmness.
- Faith can provide guidance and direction when faced with difficult decisions or challenges.
- Faith can bring comfort in times of loss or hardship and support during difficult times.
- Faith can provide a sense of purpose and meaning in life, and can help to align one's actions with one's values and beliefs.

- Faith can deepen one's spiritual connection with God, and can help to cultivate a sense of reverence, gratitude, and love.

Having faith is a personal choice, it is important to remember that faith can be strengthened through consistent practice, such as prayer, meditation, and reading religious texts. Additionally, connecting with a community of faith can be helpful. Consistent practice, such as prayer, meditation, and reading religious texts, can help to strengthen faith and deepen one's spiritual connection with their chosen deity. Being part of a community of faith can also be beneficial as it provides a supportive network of individuals who share similar beliefs and can provide guidance and encouragement. Jesus said that God the Holy Spirit will never leave believers alone.

And Jesus said to him, "Go your way; your faith has made you well". And immediately he recovered his sight and followed him on the way. (Mark 10:52)

By acknowledging Jesus as the source of our healing and restoration, we can experience transformational powers in our own lives.

The Ho'oponopono prayer:

"**I love you**" - commitment
"**Please forgive me**" - responsibility
"**I am so sorry**" - regret
"**Thank you**" - gratitude
"**Clean, clean, clean**" - purification

To finish off...

Ho'oponopono is a prayer that helps individuals align their thoughts, actions and emotions with the teachings of Jesus Christ, and become more like Him in character and spirit.

Through this process, individuals develop a deeper connection with God and gain a greater understanding of themselves and their purpose in life. This leads to a sense of inner peace, harmony and fulfilment as they live in accordance with God's will. Ho'oponopono is a spiritual practice that brings individuals closer to God and aligns them with His will. It is a way to reconnect with God and to cultivate a deeper relationship with him.

The practice helps individuals take personal responsibility for their thoughts and actions, release negative emotions, and cultivate love and compassion. This process leads to inner peace and harmony, improved relationships, physical and emotional healing, increased spiritual connection, and clarity of mind.

By placing oneself before and in the presence of God, individuals can gain a greater understanding of themselves, their purpose in life, and live in accordance with God's will. An essential part of living with God is learning how to communicate with Him. This includes learning how to listen to God, how to speak to God, and how to understand and respond to God's communication with us.

Ho'oponopono can help with this by providing a framework for understanding and expressing remorse, gratitude, and love towards God, as well as helping to clear negative thoughts and emotions that may block our ability to hear and understand God's communication with us.

Through regular practice, the Ho'oponopono prayer can deepen our spiritual connection with God and help us to live more fully in alignment with His will and purpose for our lives. It can also help us to develop a deeper understanding of ourselves, our relationships with others, and the role that we play in the world. Additionally, it can help us to let go of negative thoughts, emotions and past traumas, which can free us from being stuck in the past and allow us to move forward in a positive direction. Ultimately, Ho'oponopono can help us to become more loving, compassionate and peaceful individuals, which can lead to a greater sense of inner peace and fulfilment.

> **"The inner presence of God, brought to us by the Spirit, is meant to transform us"** *(Francis MacNutt, 2006)*

Communicating with God through the prayer of Ho'oponopono is not only about gaining knowledge and understanding, but also about developing a deeper relationship with God. It helps us to become more in tune with God's will and purpose for our lives, and to live in alignment with those principles. Through regular practice, we can deepen our spiritual connection with God and build a stronger foundation for our faith. This can lead to a greater sense of inner peace, harmony, and fulfilment in our lives as we become more closely aligned with God's will.

> ***In him we have redemption through his blood, the forgiveness of sins, in accordance with the riches of God's grace that he lavished on us with all wisdom and understanding.*** (Ephesians 1:7-8 NIV)
>
> All have sinned and fall short of His glory, it is only through Jesus that we have a way to have salvation. We have been forgiven, we have been redeemed.

Ho'oponopono is a way to cleanse ourselves of negative thoughts and emotions that can block this reconciliation and to open ourselves up to the love and guidance of God. Through regular practice, we can deepen our spiritual connection with God and live more fully in alignment with his will and purpose for our lives. It is a way to seek forgiveness continuously and to strive to live a more Christ-like life. It helps us to stay connected with God, to hear his voice and to follow his guidance.

> ***He has given us his very great and precious promises, so that through them you may participate in the divine nature, having escaped the corruption in the world caused by evil desires.*** (2 Peter 1:4 NIV)
>
> We know that a promise is a declaration of certainty, with eternal currency, a tangible gift.

So, what has God promised us?

- Eternity within His family
- An end to our suffering
- Transformation through the power of the Holy Spirit
- Purpose and meaning everlasting

Right now we can start on that road. Regardless of where we are on our spiritual journey, Ho'oponopono can be an effective tool for helping us to start, and deepen our connection with God, and for learning how to communicate with him more effectively. Through regular practice, we can learn to release negative emotions and take personal responsibility for our thoughts and actions. This can lead to inner peace and harmony, improved relationships, physical and emotional healing, and increased spiritual connection.

Additionally, by listening to God and following our intuition, we can stay connected with God and live more fully in alignment with his will and purpose for our lives. Ultimately, walking with God and reaching a settled, abiding communion and fellowship with him is the goal of all Christian life, and Ho'oponopono can be an important step on this journey.

Come to me, all you who are weary and burdened, and I will give you rest. (Matthew 11:28)

Jesus is inviting us to experience the love of God, which is demonstrated through His Son's sacrifice on the cross. By coming to Him, we can receive His assurance of eternal life with Him. Jesus is inviting us to come and see who He is and what He has done for us. He is inviting us to come and experience a personal relationship with Him. All we have to do is accept His invitation and come to Him with an open heart and mind.

Finally, everything is in God, and God is in everything. This idea is central to many spiritual traditions, which is a Christian spiritual formation movement which emphasises the growth and transformation of the whole person: body, mind, and spirit. Through Ho'oponopono and then subsequent practices such as prayer, meditation, study of scripture, and service, our relationship with God deepens and we live more fully in alignment with God's will and purpose.

By taking personal responsibility for our thoughts and actions, releasing negative emotions, and being open and receptive to God's guidance, we can achieve inner peace and harmony, improve relationships, experience physical and emotional healing, and increase our spiritual connection.

The goal of this Ho'oponopono mantra is thus to facilitate spiritual transformation and bring individuals closer to God, ultimately fostering a settled abiding communion and fellowship with God.

> *"When we begin to sense this transformation of the Spirit, this quiet, this stillness, this hope, this peace, then we begin to realise that the possessions we have valued are a weight that we need to throw off. Things begin to mean less because know we have something else – peace and liberty, a stillness, a richness of heart"* (Jean Vanier, 1975:117)

Through regular practice of Ho'oponopono, we can deepen our relationship with God and learn to hear His voice more clearly. This can lead to a greater understanding of His will and purpose for our lives, and a greater ability to obey and follow Him. By focusing on our connection with God, we can become more like Him, bearing more fruit and experiencing a deeper sense of fulfilment, joy and love. When we love unconditionally, we are able to see the best in others and in ourselves, and we are more likely to act with kindness, empathy, and compassion.

In the context of Ho'oponopono, love is a central component of the forgiveness process. By cultivating love and compassion towards oneself and others, we can release negative emotions and heal past hurts. Love can also help us to take responsibility for our actions and make amends when we have caused harm to others. In many cultures and traditions, love is regarded as the highest and most important of all human values, and it is often seen as the key to creating a harmonious and fulfilling life.

While we do not look at the things which are seen, but at the things which are not seen. For the things which are seen are temporary, but the things which are not seen are eternal. (2 Corinthians 4:18 NKJV)

Paul describes the two senses: anything that exists in this world and is visible to us will come and go very quickly; while whatever exists with God in the spiritual world will never end.

God provides the motivation, guidance and encouragement to connect with Him. All that is left is for us is to act on that decision to re-connect with Him. He provides the tools; we only need to use them. Life is so short, why not get the very best from life by re-connecting to God with the Ho'oponopono structure, and build our relationship again...we have nothing to lose, and *everything* to gain !

The Ho'oponopono prayer:

"I love you"
"Please forgive me"
"I am so sorry"
"Thank you"
"Clean, clean, clean"

References

American Psychological Association (n.d.). *APA Dictionary of Psychology*. Available from: https://dictionary.apa.org(Accessed May 1st 2023).

Atiqah, N. (2022). *The self-help industry is booming, but its advice is rarely based on solid evidence*. The Skeptic. Available from https://www.skeptic.org.uk/2022/03/the-self-help-industry-is-booming-but-its-advice-is-rarely-based-on-solid-evidence (Accessed 10th April 2023)

Brengle, S. L. (1954). *When the Holy Ghost is come*. London: Salvationist Publishers & Supplies.

Brother Lawrence (1977). *The Practice of the Presence of God.* Philadelphia: Judson.

Brother Lawrence (1977). In Foster, R. J., & Smith, J. B. (1993). *Devotional Classics: Selected Readings for Individuals and Groups*. San Francisco: Harper Collins, p.129.

Broome, J. R. (2011). *Augustus Toplady (1740-1778).* Available from: https://banneroftruth.org/uk/resources/articles/2011/augustus-toplady-1740-1778(Accessed 15th June 2023).

de Chardin, P.T. (1959). *The Phenomenon of Man.* London: Fontana Books, Collins.

Duprée, U.E. (2012). *Ho'oponopono: The Hawaiian Forgiveness Ritual as the Key to Your Life's Fulfilment*. Forres, Scotland: Findhorn Press.

Duvall, J. S. & Hays, J. D. (2020). *Grasping God's Word: A Hands-On Approach to Reading, Interpreting, and Applying the Bible.* Grand Rapids, Michigan: Zondervan Academic

Ellis, K. (2015). *One Minute with God: Sixty Super natural Seconds that will Change Your Life*. Charlotte, NC: Messianic Vision.

Ettman, C.K., Cohen, G.H., Galea, S. (2020).*Is wealth associated with depressive symptoms in the United States?* Available from: https://www.ncbi.nlm.nih.gov/pmc/articles/PMC7891298/pdf/nihms-1636826.pdf
(Accessed 2nd May 2023)

Everett, K. (2020). *A Visual Representation of the Holy trinity*. Twitter (27 May 2020).

Foster, R.J. (1992). *Prayer, Finding the Heart's True Home.* London: Hodder and Stoughton, p.89-90.

Gitnux (2023). *The Latest Self-Help Industry Statistics 2023 You Shouldn't Ignore*. Available from: www.gitnux.com (Accessed 1st May 2023).

Goeke, N. (2008).*The Secret.* Available from: https://ngoeke.medium.com/the-secret-9dc4fe57142
(Accessed 22nd March 2023).

Gooding, D. (2013). *The Riches of Divine Wisdom.* N Ireland: Myrtlefield House.

Graybeal, L. & Roller, J. (2009). *Connecting with God*. NY: HarperCollins Publishers Inc.

Graham, B. (1978). *The Holy Spirit: Activating God's Power in Your Life Paperback.* Nashville, TN: HarperCollins Christian Publishing.

Hosmanek, A.J. (2005). *Cutting the Cord: Ho'oponopono and Hawaiian Restorative Justice in the Criminal Law Context.* Available from:https://digitalcommons.pepperdine.edu/cgi/viewcontent.cgi?article=1106&context=drlj(Accessed 20th June 2023).

Jackson. P (2014). *Ho'oponopono Secrets: Four Phrases to Change the World One Love to Bind Them*. Portland, United States: Tavern Books.

Johnson, B. (2003). *When heaven invades earth: A practical guide to a life of miracles*. Shippensburg, PA: Treasure House.

Katz, M. (2010). *The Easiest Way: Solve Your Problems and Take the Road to Love, Happiness, Wealth and the Life of your Dreams*. Woodland Hills, California, US: Your Business Press.

Kempis, T. (2012). *The Imitation of Christ*. London: Burns & Oates.

Laubach, F. (1950). In Foster, R. J., & Smith, J. B. (1993). *Devotional classics: selected readings for individuals and groups.* San Francisco: Harper Collins, *p.178.*

Lennox, J. C. (2011). *Seven Days that Divide the World.* Grand Rapids, Michigan: Zondervan.

Lennox, J. C. (2017). ***Determined to Believe? Determined to Believe: The Sovereignty of God, Faith and Human Responsibility***. Oxford, UK; Monarch Books.

Lloyd-Jones, M. (2012). ***Great Doctrines of the Bible (Three Volumes in One): God the Father, God the Son; God the Holy Spirit; The Church and the Last Things.*** Wheaton, Illinois: Crossway Books.

Lloyd-Jones, M. (1993). ***Fellowship with God.*** Wheaton, Illinois: Crossway Books.

MacNutt, F. (2006). ***The healing reawakening: Reclaiming our lost inheritance.*** Grand Rapids, MI, Chosen Books.

Maldonado, G. (2011). ***Power of God: How to Walk in the Supernatural.*** New Kensington, PA: Whitaker House.

Melanie, L. (2018). ***What People are Still Willing to Pay For?*** Available: https://www.forbes.com/2009/01/15/self-help-industry-ent-sales-cx_ml_0115selfhelp.html
(Accessed 5th February, 2023).

Mercer, J. (2013). ***Intimacy with God Walking in the Holy Spirit***. Walkintheholyspirit.com.

Meyer, J. (2025). ***Closer to God Each Day: 365 Devotions for Everyday Living.*** New York: Faith Words.

Pytches, D. (1985). ***Come Holy Spirit: Learning to Minister in Power.*** London: Hodder & Stoughton.

Ruth, P. J. (2012). ***Psalm 91: God's Shield of Protection.*** Lake Mary, Florida; Creation house.

Ryu. S., &Fan, L. (2022).***The Relationship Between Financial Worries and Psychological Distress Among U.S. Adults.*** Available from: https://www.ncbi.nlm.nih.gov/pmc/articles/PMC8806009/ (Accessed 10th February 2023)

Simons, R. C. (2021). ***When Strivings Cease: Replacing the Gospel of Self-Improvement with the Gospel of Life-Transforming Grace.*** Nashville, Tennessee: Nelson Books.

Steere, D. (1938) ***Prayer and Worship.*** New York: Edward W. Hazen Foundation & Association Press.

Tari, M. (1971). In Foster, R. (1992). ***Prayer, Finding the Heart's True Home.*** London: Hodder & Stoughton, *p.126-127.*

Tristram, G. (2013). ***Reconciliation & Atonement: How God Mended a Broken World.*** Society of Saint John the Evangelist.

Tov, W. (2018). Well-being concepts & components. In ***Handbook of subjective well-being*** (pp. 1-15). Salt Lake City, UT: Noba Scholar. Available at: https://ink.library.smu.edu.sg/soss_research/2836

Vanier, J. (1975). ***Be not afraid.*** Dublin: Gill & Macmillan.

Vitale, J. (2007). ***Zero limits: The secret Hawaiian system for wealth, health, peace, and more.*** Hew Len, Haleakalā. Hoboken, N.J.: Wiley.

Warren, R. (2002). ***The Purpose Driven Life: What on Earth Am I Here For?*** Grand Rapids, Michigan: Zondervan.

White, E, G. (1955). ***Sons and Daughters of God.*** Washington, D.C.: Herald Publishing Association.

Wigglesworth, S. (1940). ***Smith Wigglesworth Quotes by Mark Conely.*** (Accessed YouTube, Aug 2005)

www.ingramcontent.com/pod-product-compliance
Lightning Source LLC
Chambersburg PA
CBHW041144110526
44590CB00027B/4123